MICHAEL E. ABERSON

ECONOMIC BEHAVIOR MODEL
AND VOLTAGE PATTERN
(MACROSOFT PROTOCOL BASE)

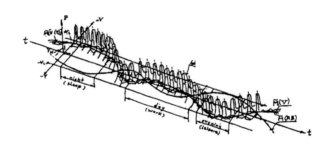

CAMBRIDGE

MELROSE BOOKS

2008

Published by

**MELROSE
BOOKS**

An Imprint of Melrose Press Limited
St Thomas Place, Ely
Cambridgeshire
CB7 4GG, UK
www.melrosebooks.com

FIRST EDITION

Library of the US Congress (Copyright Number: TXu-464-775)

ISBN 978 1 906050 13 9

Printed and bound in Great Britain by:
Biddles 24 Rollesby Road, Hardwick Industrial Estate
King's Lynn. Norfolk PE30 4LS

Winston S. Churchill

Never give in if you are
the serious professional.
W. Churchill, 1941

GENERAL CONCLUSIONS: CANONIC IT FOR MACROECONOMY

1. The world sound economy is a newest Cadillac...with false mirrors, i.e., with <u>false information technology</u> (IT). That's industrial management update central gap.

2. There are 4 critical problems in industrial <u>macroeconomy</u>:

<u>uncertain investment forecasting</u> that is a vast waste of time and money;

<u>false feedback</u> from end user that is the main obstacle for quality progress;

<u>inflexibility</u> of industrial, financial and social rates;

<u>the dead contradiction</u>: public responsibilities – private interests.

3. <u>"ELECTRONIC WHEEL" or "ECONOMIC WHEEL"</u> <u>cybernetical digital IT (EWIT</u> protocol) is the only digital patent to solve critical problems above (founded on 3D Economic Behavior Model: Macrosoft Protocol Base) nearly to the true optimum in 5-7 years.

4. Technotronic era proper embodiment needs 2 tough divided basic approaches:

PC-zation for <u>microeconomy</u> with <u>personal</u> softwares (20% of GDP): E-mail, culture, retailing, education, science, design, medicine, police, bank, office documentation, children's games; <u>Internet;</u>

EW-zation for industrial <u>macroeconomy</u> with <u>standard</u> software/digital code (80% of GDP): production/service <u>business units which operate 24 hours a day</u>): raw materials, fuel, energy, water, food, capital, labor, social, transport, environmental, short and long term strategy with rat race for mainframe computer and min-min "human factor" impact (only for strategic decision-making based on <u>stochastic-discrete-measured information</u>); <u>Cybernet.</u>

4

5. EWIT is distributed data coding fully automated micro-processor-based IT with raw metering <u>data input</u> (for resources, processes and feedback) and behavioristicic object-oriented, real time open protocol (digital data output); only two classic linear procedures (simplex and/or regression) are used for each 6-hour data file with local social optimum (night/blue, morning/white, afternoon/gray, evening/pink); EWIT protocol is the final breakthrough for industrial macroeconomy's management update and productivity growth.

6. EWIT protocol main economic and social benefits for each line production/service:

1) No less than 9÷15% costs saving, for every one $1 billion of sales (GDP); it depends on metrology base development.

2) Standard 6-hour working day or about 20% new jobs for industrial countries: <u>unemployment problem is removing from the desk</u>. <u>Privacy-Work balance is close to the limit.</u>

7. "<u>Personal Factor</u>" (education, new breed of executives, skilled managers and programmers, special training, workstations, etc.) is NOT a key to the survival of a line industrial <u>macroeconomy</u> as the large object for automation. <u>Personal emphasis is a pace loss</u>.

8. <u>EWIT complete meets N. Wiener's prophetical requirements to "taping machines" and the behavioristic concept as a whole; he is staying the expert N1</u>.

9. <u>EWIT standardization is an imperative task for IEEE and ISO</u>.

References:

1. Theory "Economic Behavior Model and Voltage Pattern" (Macrosoft Protocol Base)

2. EWIT protocol (US Patents: 5,515,288; 5,732,193; 08/035,699 (pending).

Michael E. Aberson, P.E., Ph.D.
EWIT inventor

ECONOMIC BEHAVIOR MODEL AND VOLTAGE PATTERN
(MACROSOFT PROTOCOL BASE)

ABSTRACT

This monograph discusses the central problems of the Neumann – Morgenstern and Wiener studies (1943 – 48) – the building of a formalized model of economic/rational behavior (RB) and customer feedback: a conceptual database for macrobusiness management, quality, communication and control. "Economic Behavior Model and Voltage Pattern" is the statistical-economic study of the modern phenomenon of human behavior, both individuals and society as a whole. The statistical tool is tolerant AC service voltage statistical-economic ratings at the sale, i.e., under electrical meter sockets – the subject point of this essential and versatile commodity's exchange for two classic players of commercial "risk": the monopole supplier and an ignorant user. The voltage paradox stochastic idea is the only successful clue to the dual canonic digital solution of the Neumann – Morgenstern and Wiener's today central problems:

- The 3-D discrete stochastic model of RB;
- Probabilistic stability (feedback) verification of model or the "axiomatic treatment of utility."

These two scientific results are the basis of the "Stability and Utility" engineering "macrosoft" concept, which is the background of EWIT protocol ("electronic wheel" information technology): the 3D linear-discrete stochastic model's full digital software embodiment (which is contained in US patents: 5,515,288; 5,732,193; S/N08,035,699 pending). It means the historical transfer to the new standard industrial datamation (digital automation protocol version) with great benefits for macroeconomic production and service. Pg. 150, Fig. 17, Tb. 8.

Dedicated to remarkable electrical engineers, N. Tesla and J. Chervonenkis: they were plotting the unique way to measurement-based cybertech digital protocol for each macrobusiness data (resources, processes and feedback).

CONTENTS

PREFACE

*T*his concise monograph has been specifically written for
the qualified reader: product manager, control engineer,
serious economist, and astrophysicist. Unfortunately, it reflects the author's engineering snobbery, containing only
the necessary material for an effective behavioristic model
construction. If more attention were paid to describing the
problems of "arm-chair" intellectuals, this book would
weigh three times as much.

Modern business strives to overcome one central dilemma: how to achieve high quality at low cost. This
eternal economic dilemma has been theoretically resolved
here for the stable recurrent business, specifically, macrobusiness (which operates 24 hours a day), as a clean
cybernetical-system dynamic object. It is clear from the
quote above this preface that as far back as 180 AD, em-
peror-stoic Marcus Aurelius already knew what would be
considered a "top secret" for some contemporary "chaos
consultants": Nature is a system.

As a fundamental behavioristic function, we use a
conceptual AC "Voltage Paradox," which is the only path to
satisfactory statistical-economic research (Chapter 1). Behavioristic model's problem could not be resolved for over
two hundred years because the only valid tool for its study
is monopole-supplied AC electricity's distribution to each
end user. Indeed, there is a unique opportunity (the gift of

N. Tesla): A pure physical function (AC service voltage) now completely represents an essential day-to-day commodity's exchange and its marginal-cardinal-ordinal utility within tolerant-statistical ratings. These ratings ($\pm$ V_N, %) are true integral criteria of commercial equilibrium (quality of exchange) in an elementary incessant day-to-day "two-person game": the monopole supplier and an illiterate purchaser (end user).

The 3D formalized linear-discrete model of rational behavior (Chapter 2) and its axiomatic utility treatment (Chapter 3) are the probabilistic-stochastic base for a concluding "Stability and Utility" engineering concept as the standard digital discrete "macrosoftware" social base for a cybertech fully-automated digital protocol version (the initial "astronomic" postulate and twelve practical axioms (Chapter 4) [1].

Concluding remarks (Chapter 5) and a bibliography reveal the measure of our confusion and misunderstanding when confronted with such a long and sad story of contradictions and innocent partialities in human-made theories that, we hope, have been properly examined by a practical electrical engineer.

Therefore, to gain a well-rounded understanding of the nontrivial approach to classical economic notions, which is presented here, one needs to read (at least as a primer), the initial sections of the almost completely forgotten works by J. von Neumann, O. Morgenstern, N. Wiener, J. Forrester and C. Bary.

---

[1] The semantic approach here means two different fields in cybernetic sense: macro- and microbusinesses or the general digital software/code ("macrosoft") and various personal softwares ("microsoft").

It seems strange that only Americans (including T. Veblen, and G. Dantzig) appear on this short, remarkable list. As a profound economic confirmation of our cybernetic-system approach to social life, we consider *Capitalism and Freedom* by M. Friedman.

We believe that if our approach is correct, this monograph can be considered as a final chapter of the collective study initiated by J. von Neumann in 1928.

The results of this "final chapter" are briefly summarized in section 5.6 (Valid Results). This represents a radical turn from the "monotheistic trust" in *personal* subjective relationships and *personal* intuitive preferences which are used in classical theory as the main subject matter for making money. This "personal" philosophy remains true, but now it is a secondary factor mainly in microbusiness for a free postindustrial society.

The crucial factor for 3D complex line macro business (production and service companies) in the technotronic era is an adequate fully automatic canonic datamation or the measurement-based social economy with standard linear-discrete digital communication, computing and control protocol based on standard software/digital code. In this case, the entropy gradient or an unbalanced dynamic state of the world will have a moderate, less tight spiral.

ACKNOWLEDGEMENTS

A true co-author of this monograph could be the late (1916 – 1970) Dr. J. Chervonenkis (Academy of Municipal Economy, Moscow).

Appendices in Chapters 2 and 3 were resolved with the

great support of prominent scholars in the random theory such as Acad. V. Pugachov, Dr. L. Sisoyev, Acad. B. Gnedenko and Prof. A. Soloview (Institute of Control Problems and Moscow State University).

An engineering guide by Prof. A. Pervozvanski (Leningrad Polytechnic Institute) has helped me to understand that cybernetics in **macroeconomy** is a fully independent field.

Haifa, 2004

CHAPTER 1

AC Electricity – Statistical Medium

> There are many economists who object that economic theory can be modelled after physics since it is a science of social and human phenomenon and has to take psychology into account. Such statements are at least premature. There is a little hope that model will be settled by the usual methods during our lifetime.
>
> Statistical-economic research holds the real promise in the proper direction.
>
> *J. von Neumann,*
> *O. Morgenstern, 1944*
>
> Statistics needed an adequate philosophic background.
>
> *I. Good, 1990*

1.1 The Basic Commodity

Today, words like "Electricity is critical to economic health; its versatility makes it an essential commodity" seem rather banal [1]. More interesting, however, is the following: "Many see equal long-term annual growth for both GNP and electricity. All sectors are expected to use significantly more electricity by the year 2000" [1].

M. Friedman's statement regarding the nature of progress over the past century is to the point: "Medicine aside, the advances in technology have for the most part simply made available to the masses *of the people luxuries* that were always available in one form or another to the truly wealthy. Modern plumbing, central heating, automobiles, television, radio – to cite just a few examples – provide conveniences to the masses equivalent to those that the wealthy could always get by the use of servants, entertainers, and so on"[9]. It would be an accurate addition to say that AC electricity looms behind of all these *luxuries*.

The decisive role of AC electricity (in living standards, industry, services, science, etc.) in the GDP growth of developed society is virtually beyond debate. Equally obvious is the connection of electricity with the rational behavior of an individual (for example, Edison's light bulb and the radical change in the sleep/leisure time span ratio). Other features of AC electricity as affecting a professional, however, are likewise banal:

a) The creation of a new value (product), unlike natural water, gas and some other products (air, blood, fruits, etc.)[2];
b) The simultaneity of production and consumption;
c) The impossibility of storage (unlike water, gas and other products);
d) The irregular, with different power, random demand (beyond the ordered queue theory);
e) The security problem (safety, reliability, and quality).

It is appropriate to note here that econometrics considers an electrical power system as a typical "national monopoly" whose goal is "marginal peak load pricing" and other "marginal benefits" [20]. Its key words are "regulation" and "commission" (as a means to "curb" the monopoly). Various meters and TOU (time of use) tariffs basically serve to extract "marginal benefits" from the consumer's pocket (taking into account

---

[2] T. Edison was the first to see a young "green" menace to his DC love and money: the 10-year battle was furious. Fortunately for everyone, the true spirit of innovation (instead of rituals) was alive one hundred years ago: G. Westinghouse and N. Tesla won the Niagara station contract. However, it is correct that the AC sinusoidal product has no analog in Nature, the same as a wheel.

his interests). However, the troubles of modern power systems (shareholders' dividend decline in spite of huge annual capital investment in advanced high-tech equipment; full automation and computerization, mainly, PC-zation) indicate the futility of the traditional marginal approach to electricity as an eternal win-win business. Nevertheless, power systems are now under tremendous pressure from many public sources to become more efficient and productive (under tough pollution regulations too).

The fundamental "silent" problem – *utility or quality of AC electricity for the consumer*, due to specific commodity features (danger and impalpability) – remains in essence "terra incognita." Such "visible" AC disturbances as flicker, spikes, sugs, and harmonic distortions have been considered, for many years, as AC electricity basic quality units. The widespread introduction of electronic loads serves as a reason for AC electricity quality "improvement" from the commercial perspective – the one-sided demand of "power conditioner" manufacturers (UPS and others), and/or both supply-demand side program – as a purely academic answer to this industry's troubles (Least Cost Planning, Demand Side Management, etc.).

The material presented here is an attempt to consider more deeply the unique qualitative features of AC electricity, including its statistical nature, as an essential commodity. And indeed – if AC electricity is fully involved today in GDP formation, *is it possible to use its phenomenon as a versatile informational and economic medium*, as a specific cybertech-substance for the instrumental analysis of a rational agent's behavior and its group as a whole? This is the key question.

There are two recognized formulations for this conceptual question:

(1) Human society is a statistical law phenomenon (N. Wiener) [3].

(2) Economics is a nonexperimental discipline (L. Klein) [10].

Our approach to this question follows (1). As it turns out, AC electricity is possible *and, moreover, it is the only successful approach to the development of a formalized model of economic (rational) behavior.*

1.2 The "Voltage Paradox"

The commodity properties of AC electricity as a propagating medium are considered below:

(**1**) *A centralized form of delivery and an individual form of consumption.*

One must profoundly grasp the close correlation of an independent "on-off" decision with the rational and emotional behavior of an individual or a group, i.e., between decision making and electricity's utility. An on-off act (e.g., lighting TV, VCR, OO, PC, mixer, etc.) is also a *private-free* act of the everyday "buy-sell" electrical supply process in which the player's judgments as a rule are completely isolated, including his "*moral expectation.*"

Ohm's law ($i = u/r$), a fundamental law of electrotechnology, is a fully-fledged logical and physical analog of the causal relationship between the quantity of this commodity (through changes of current, i) and the quality (utility) of this commodity (through changes of voltage, u).

The stochastic on-off function of the lighting, TV, PC, VCR, electric kettle, machine tool, videogame machine, etc. is fully and closely related to the social *biorhythm* of modern civilization [3].

(**2**) *Repetitiveness, that is, a "millions of events per day," and thus each day.*

---

[3] We think that with the help of AC electricity it is possible to measure the Bentham categories and even to write two scientific treatises: "On the utility of suffering and the disutility of good" or "On the utility of good and the disutility of suffering."

The scale of sampling is utterly inaccessible to the Gallup or Yankelovich polls, for example. *Repetitiveness is the heart of economic activity, the essence of producing a value.* We cannot help citing here the incisive words of von Neumann – Morgenstern: "Only prolonged [stellar dynamic] observations of Tycho de Brahe gave rise to Kepler and Newton [and not the famous apple – *M.A.*]. It would have been absurd in physics to expect Kepler and Newton without Tycho" [2].

(<u>3</u>) *Extremely high "value in use" and extremely low "value in exchange" (as in air, water and bread); this is explained by its purity, impalpability, high efficiency and simplicity of distribution* [4].

(<u>4</u>) *Equal level of utility (quality criteria) under centralized supply, which ensures the strictness of statistical data processing.*

This factor is valid due to the presence of only two criteria: standard *frequency* and *voltage level*. These two criteria are basic rates for electrical power system stability (dynamic and steady-state).

(<u>5</u>) *An enormous and diverse market of goods which uses electricity in all phases and modes of rational behavior, i.e., an equipotential field of statistical inquiry* [5].

(<u>6</u>) *The "flip-flop" principle of preference revelation, which is important for statistical research reliability of results.*

As in computers, this is the basis of a proper digital procedure. At the same time, it provides a *probabilistic combination*

---

[4] This is a secret of electricity's *versatility* in all realms of modern activity, i.e., its *statistical reliability* as an information medium.
[5] Electricity/commodity is immune to slack or stagnant demand; it always outruns production.

of both types of behavior: "choice under certainty" and "choice under uncertainty." The flip-flop principle of preference revelation means a *fundamental silent fact*: frequency approximation to decision-making probability. We do not see any particular expediency in the formal Bayesian approach to this model.

Theoretically, the *Bayesian probability* impact is beyond an argument. *Practically speaking*, however, ("millions of events per day"), it seems like an unjustified overindulgence, complicating the analysis, which is not simple to begin with. This is even more true for the instrumental statistical analysis, which silently reflects Bayesian law. I. Good and P. Fishburn provide a close commentary to the point [27].

(<u>7</u>)   *Coincidence of the 24-hour calendar day with the electricity consumption pattern and with the human activity social biorhythm cycle* [6].

Thus, we do not know of any other commodity that is as universal as AC electricity for the instrumental and theoretical study of the humanoid's rational behavior [7].

All that remains is to answer precisely *why AC service voltage stochastic function at the delivery* is the only informational and economic medium for an adequate statistical message; or, *why the voltage paradox is the only valid tool for this statistical-economic research?* There are several reasons for this:

(<u>1</u>)   Unlike the tough frequency criterion, empirical international norms of AC tolerant voltage deviations from the

---

[6] J. Hicks' well-known statement, "Trade takes place weekly," seems fully intuitive. J. Jewons was closer to the main point when discussing solar spots and crop yield [14].

[7] In contrast to the generally accepted terms, "end user", "individual", "rational agent," "person" or "client," we sometimes use the term *humanoid* (as a being with a subconsciousness).

nominal at sale ($\pm V_N$, %) are marked by statistical content. They have no rigorous analytical base, but contain fundamental "exchange" meaning. They reflect the almost *100-year commercial experience of the centralized electrical supply. Exactly because of AC service voltage ratings' statistical content, we use the apparatus of the random theory*, that is apparently the only relevant statistical tool for our study.

(2)   One can confidently consider the steady-state voltage limits as an integral criterion because *they reflect the economic compromise* or game between supplier and consumer, their contract commercial equilibrium (equal risk).

(3)   The function of utility (or damage) follows *square dependence* in the vicinity of the voltage tolerant norms ($\pm V_N$) [19].

Insofar as AC electricity is an essential commodity, it means that the numerical assessment of utility, i.e., the mathematical expectation (level) of AC voltage at delivery, is adequate for the mathematical expectation of rational behavior intensity (i.e., to its model life-line validity).

(4)   The state metrology service for electrical quantities uses "volt" as a basic standard unit.

Thus the *voltage paradox (AC service voltage stochastic function) is a unique statistical tool for a formalized model of rational behavior building* [8].

---

[8] 1. AC *current* reflects only the quantitative (marginal) aspect of exchange (through a tariff). It is a less informative parameter than voltage for econometric philosophy (as a quality aspect of exchange).

2. Centralized supply of AC electricity is a classic problem of commercial inequality between monopoly and a solitary end user. Impalpability of electricity (absence of its quality control at the moment payment is made)

Summing up, one can confidently consider AC service voltage ratings at the sale as a unique "polyhedron" of information, on whose facets the basic economic categories are "inscribed" every minute by the individual: utility and probability, rationality, maximum strategy, planning, certainty and uncertainty, risk, preference, psychology relevant opportunity, decision making rules, stochastic dominance, confident commodity, etc.

So perfect a medium of economic information as the Voltage Paradox can be compared to a die, serving as the foundation for the Laplas and Bernoulli *monument* – the Probabilities theory [9].

---

increases the inequality of the consumer. "Regulation" and "commission" cannot limit this specific *supplier's silent right* of "the first night." The only proper solution is "customer feedback information" (N. Wiener's requirement in the ISO-9004 standard).

[9] The centralized "monopoly" of AC electrical supply presents a successful opportunity for resolving the Neumann – Morgenstern classic problem. We anticipate [13] a dramatic transition *to decentralized electrical supply* by local fuel cells in the 21st century (for ecological reasons) and thus to Thomas Edison, Werner von Siemens, and Lord Kelvin's favorite – DC as the dominant electricity. In that case, the development of the rational behavior model will finally become unattainable.

CHAPTER 2
3-D Stochastic V≡RB Model

> It is necessary to know as much as
> possible about the behavior of the in-
> dividual and about the simplest forms
> of exchange.
>
> *J. von Neumann, O. Morgenstern, 1944*

2.1 Definitions

It was assumed that:

(1)   The operation of one electrical receiver (**R**) is the result of one humanoid's (**H**) behavior (**R≡H**);

(2)   The operation of a *group* of electrical receivers is the result of an independent *group*'s behavior (**GR≡GH**);

(3)   The behavior of the stochastic AC service voltage function (**V**) at delivery (given standard utility) and its characteristics are fully adequate for the properties of the rational behavior (**RB**) model (**V≡RB**). This definition follows from (1) and (2)[10].

The **V≡RB** function (e.g., in urban electrical networks) due to the random character of independent **R≡H** (**GR≡GH**) activity is a stochastic process similar to the Markovian chains. Its partial description, which is sufficient for our analysis, is given by the function F(x,t) in the form:

$$F(x, t) = \int_{-\infty}^{x} p(u, t)dt \qquad (1)$$

---

[10] This basic maximum likelihood approach is possible due to the remarkable statistical-economic properties of the voltage paradox (see Chapter 1).

Two basic problems must be resolved through the measured stochastic process model. It is necessary to define:

(1) *The class of the random process* (stationary hypothesis verification);

(2) *The proper law approximation of an instantaneous (fixed) density for* p (u,t).

The second problem has not been considered in any of the known works on the voltage stochastic function. Its solution by means of the instrumental approach is impractical; it can only be accomplished analytically. It is based on the classic work by S. Rice [4], who developed a probabilistic model by the characteristic functions method for the electrons shot effect.

The fact that the $\mathbf{V} \equiv \mathbf{RB}$ stochastic function can be considered the sum of a number of isolated operations (independent decisions) assumes an *a priori* possibility of the process approximation by Gaussian law. We find it difficult, however, in this case to verify the conditions of the Liapunov central limiting theorem due to the essentially *varying intensity and power of this process*. Herein lies the principal difference between our analysis and S. Rice's approach. Taking into account the varying rational intensity as an inevitable feature of the physical nature of the $\mathbf{V} \equiv \mathbf{RB}$ model, its profound divergence from the classical stochastic processes (stellar dynamics, Brownian motion, etc.) can be noted [4].

Substantiation, which is based on the Muavr – Laplas asymptotic formula for the binomial law case, is also unconvincing. Indeed, some fluctuations of the $\mathbf{V} \equiv \mathbf{RB}$ realization cannot be presented in the form $\mathbf{m} \cdot \mathbf{U}°$, where $\mathbf{m}$ = number of electrical receivers (or independent decisions), and $\mathbf{U}°$ = voltage drop as a result of individual behavior.

The main feature of the electrical receivers is a power variety under full stochastic-behavioristic impact. This makes it essentially different from the ordered queue theory apparatus. Furthermore, the electrical receivers' state is also different at every moment (on-off distribution). These two differences serve as a basis for the close correlation and *similarity between the voltage pattern development process and the economic (rational) behavior or independent decisions (individual or group)*, i.e., the statistical base of the **V≡RB** probabilistic model[11,12].

2.2 Experimental Stationary Hypothesis Verification

The class of the stochastic process (stationary or time-dependent) determines one of the key questions for its reliable probabilistic model development and its adequate analysis (instrumental and in applications). The **V≡RB** function at some point of the hyperspace phase can be presented in the following canonic form:

$$(V≡RB) = M(t) + X^0(t), \tag{2}$$

where

M(t) – mathematical expectation ("valid signal"): an average voltage at the same moment for a number of calendar days.

---

[11] A Muavr – Laplas asymptotic approximation is acceptable, when probability is close to 0.5. It is essentially unacceptable if probability is close to 0.0 or 1.0. One can ascertain closeness of this approximation to the frequency approach as well.

[12] Little's theorem does not work here because demand delay and intensivity limit notions are beyond the electrical supply process [23].

$\mathbf{X^0(t)}$ – centered function with zero mean value; it describes the effect of "random noises"[13].

The stationary hypothesis is verified through an empirical quantitative assessment of $\mathbf{M(t)}$ and the impact of random noises $\mathbf{X^0(t)}$ on the social interval, which is equal to the stochastic biorhythm cycle, i.e., the 24-hour calendar day (during a number of days for sampling). An experimental statistical study is based on the $\mathbf{V \equiv RB}$ function registration, measured at two points of urban electrical networks (points of commercial contract responsibility for two "players": electrical meter sockets) on the group levels $\mathbf{(GR \equiv GH)}$: (1) urban substation and (2) lead in a house[14]. Thus, stationary hypothesis verification has been performed by two independent treatment methods: the Chebyshev moments (Table 1) and the correlation matrix construction (standard programming procedure). Fig. 1 shows an original instrumental record of the $\mathbf{V \equiv RB}$ stochastic function behavior measurement by voltmeter (class 1.0) during a calendar day (an example)[15]. The sampling time span was 10-12 calendar days.

Joint consideration of Table 1 and the correlation matrices yields the following conclusions:

(1) Orders of variance $[\mathbf{D(t)}]$ in both treatments are close, which indicates the correct processing of instrumental data;

---

[13] This formulation (2) reflects the classic physical approach to stochastic signals, based on Langevin's equation: $\mathbf{du/dt = -\beta u + A(t)}$ [4].

[14] An example of the statistical processing is provided in Appendix 2.1. Correlation matrices of the $\mathbf{V \equiv RB}$ function is also given there (A2.1 - Tables 2 and 3).

[15] As a rule, professionals prefer an original signal's tidy record for a valid analysis, much more than its "blind" digital table.

Figure 1

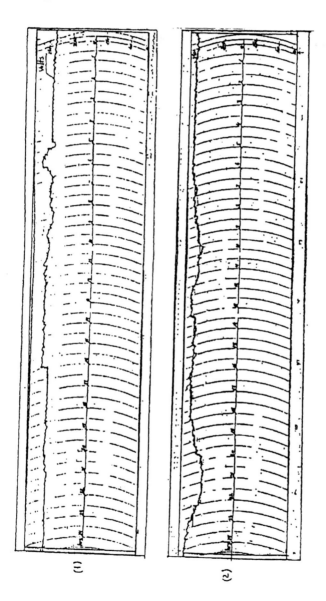

Fig. 1 Instrumental record of AC phase voltage (speed: 20mm/hr) in two group exchange points/electrical meter sockets: (1) urban substation and (2) lead-in house (118 apt). Examples.

TABLE 1
Numerical Characteristics of 24-hour V≡RB sampling
by Chebyshev method, (%)*

Point 1 (urban substation)			Point 2 (lead-in house)		
Time interval			Time interval		
(hr)	M[u(t)]	σ [u(t)]	(hr)	M [u(t)]	σ [u(t)]
			0-1	104.4	1.58
$T_1$0-1	101.4	0.92	T_1 1-2	105.1	1.15
1-2	101.4	0.94	2-3	105.2	1.18
2-3	101.25	1.02	3-4	106.0	1.18
3-4	101.75	0.97	4-5	105.0	1.12
4-5	101.3	0.95	5-6	105.9	1.12
5-6	101.5	1.33	6-7	105.0	1.82
6-7	103.2	0.71	7-8	104.6	1.46
7-8	103.0	1.17	8-9	103.0	1.31
8-9	102.4	0.96			
$T_2$9-10	103.6	1.11	$T_2$9-10	102.1	1.36
10-11	103.2	1.0	10-11	103.2	1.35
11-12	104.0	0.98	11-12	102.6	1.32
12-13	103.2	0.96	12-13	104.0	1.28
13-14	103.0	1.01	13-14	103.0	1.39
14-15	103.4	1.01	14-15	103.1	1.31

15-16	104.0	1.02			
16-17	103.4	0.85	15-16	102.8	1.33
17-18	102.25	1.4	16-17	102.1	1.27
			17-18	100.3	1.28
			18-19	99.5	1.72
T_3 18-19	101.7	1.28	T_3 19-20	98.2	1.92
19-20	101.8	1.37	20-21	99.3	1.94
20-21	101.6	1.21	21-22	101.2	1.86
21-22	102.0	1.24	22-23	99.5	1.87
22-23	102.0	1.19			
23-24	101.2	0.58	23-24	101.9	1.63

*(%)–criteria index of phase AC service voltage utility at delivery (U_N-100%)

(2) The numerical parameters of the **V≡RB** function vary; over diagonal sections in correlated matrices they are also nonuniform. These indications strengthen the hypothesis of **V≡RB** process explicit time-dependence (non-stationary) within the 24-hour social biorhythm cycle (calendar day);

(3) At the same time, there are stochastic intervals within the 24-hour cycle, when numerical parameters change insignificantly (if singled out graphically). Clearly, their duration approximately coincides with typical intervals of the daily pattern of electrical load and the daily social biorhythm cycle intervals: night (sleep), day (work), evening (leisure). This partial stability of the **V≡RB** function makes it possible to classify them as relative stationary stochastic intervals.

These results suggest a preliminary hypothesis of the *sampled non-stationary nature of the* $V{\equiv}RB$ *stochastic process in the 24-hour social biorhythm (rational behavior) cycle*. In order to strictly corroborate this hypothesis, one has to prove the unsteadiness measure of the quantitative assessment of numerical parameters by means of the error theory criteria. On the basis of averaged and asymptotically unbiased assessments, the following inequalities were obtained:

(Point 1 - urban substation)

$$\left.\begin{array}{l} \bar{M}_{T_1} + 6\bar{\sigma}_{(T_1)} < \bar{M}_{T_2} - 7\bar{\sigma}_{(T_2)}; \\ \bar{M}_{T_3} + 4\bar{\sigma}_{(T_3)} < \bar{M}_{T_2} - 4\bar{\sigma}_{(T_2)}; \end{array}\right\} \tag{3}$$

(Point 2 - lead-in house)

$$\left.\begin{array}{l} \bar{M}_{T_1} + 5\bar{\sigma}_{(T_1)} < \bar{M}_{T_2} - 5\bar{\sigma}_{(T_2)} > \bar{M}_{T_2} + 11\bar{\sigma}_{(T_2)}; \\ \bar{M}_{T_2} + 4\bar{\sigma}_{(T_3)} < \bar{M}_{T_2} - 5\bar{\sigma}_{(T_2)}; \end{array}\right\} \tag{4}$$

$$\left.\begin{array}{l} D^*_{T_1} + 4\bar{\sigma}_0 \,[D^*_{T_1}] < D^*_{T_2} - 4\bar{\sigma}_0 \,[D^*_{T_2}] < D^*_{T_3} - 6\bar{\sigma}_0 \,[D^*_{T_3}]; \\ D^*_{T_2} - 4\bar{\sigma}_0 \,[D^*_{T_2}] < D^*_{T_3} - 4\bar{\sigma}_0 \,[D^*_{T_3}]; \end{array}\right\} \tag{5}$$

where

T_1, T_2, T_3 - intervals of relative stationary of the $V{\equiv}RB$ process: night (sleep), day (work), evening (leisure).

As long as there are 4σ (rms) or more, one can claim with a confident probability of more than 0.999, that the $V{\equiv}RB$ stochastic process for group rational behavior ($GR \equiv GH$) is *an essential time-dependent (non-stationary) function* within the 24-hour social biorhythm cycle (a calendar day).

From this result, it follows that this cycle cannot be described as a single distribution density by elementary on-off (buy-sell) acts-decisions probabilities. Only a sequence of probability densities, constructed for each individual moment, can present an essential time-dependent stochastic process[16].

As our analysis has shown, however, that the presence in the 24-hour social biorhythm cycle of *several intervals* (T_1, T_2, T_3) — which can be approximated to a stationary process *preserves saves this deadlock situation*; it means the acceptance of the averaging of numerical parameters (**M, D, σ**) *on these relatively stable stochastic intervals*, which coincide with stable social segments of the daily cycle (night, day, evening; or sleep, work, leisure).

It is important to point to the basic physical feature of the given **V≡RB** process: *a slowly changing random signal with a low frequency spectrum of components*. Reliability of the correlation function is ensured by treatment of four or five of the 24-hour cycles: *the minimal duration of continuous treatment is no more than 120-130 hours*. It has also been established that the ergodic hypothesis for the **V≡RB** stochastic process is correct (Fig. 2). $\rho(\tau)$ damping indicates the ergodicity of the process. The absence of the constant components and periodicity $\rho(\tau)$ also can be noted as evidence of normalized conditions and stochastic singularity-*non-stationary*.

---

[16] The same problem arises, for example, in statistical process control, which is used in some industries.

Figure 2

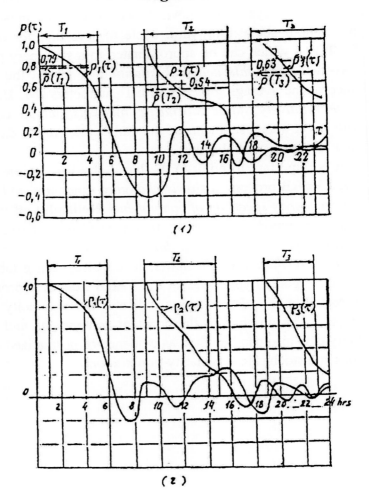

Fig. 2 Original measured V≡RB empirical correlation functions in points (1) and (2) with relative stationarity intervals (T_1, T_2, T_3).

The same conclusions also have been obtained for other urban electrical network points of the V≡RB function registration and statistical analysis (hospital, shopping center, and factory).

2.3 Analytical Approximation for Instantaneous Density

Taking into account the discussion in section 2.1 above, the present study concentrates on distribution of the **V≡RB** sto-chastic process *at a fixed moment* in some urban electrical network points of commercial exchange (e.g., electric meter sockets). Let us assume, for a given point (without any load), an initial measured voltage steady-state level U^0 which is a nominal level $(U^0 = U_N)$[17].

Furthermore, individual electrical receivers or independent hu-manoids (**R≡H**) are connected at random moments t_1, t_2,..., t_3 within a certain time interval [0,T]. The switching on-off exchange process of each **R≡H** (as a fully independent act) leads to a drop in voltage, which manifests itself in a rectangular function of time subtracted from the steady-state limit U^0 (Fig. 3).

The rectangular single voltage drop exists in the follow-ing form:

$$U^J_\theta(T\text{-}t_j) = u_jE(T\text{-}t_j) - u_jE(T\text{-}\theta\text{-}t_j), \tag{6}$$

where

t_j – moment of j-th **R≡H** connection;
θ – duration of active states each **R≡H**;
u_j – magnitude of each **R≡H** voltage drop;
$E(t)$ – unit functions[18]:
$$0 \text{ when } t < 0/1 \text{ when } t > 0 \tag{7}$$

---

[17] It is assumed, too, that the electrical system is in a stable nontransient state (frequency and impedances are constant).

[18] $E(t) = \int_{-\infty}^{t} \delta(t)$ describes the "flip-flop" effect ($\delta(t)$ – Dirac function).

We emphasize (see Chapter 1) that a *real physical effect of voltage drop is a visible measured "rectangular" statistical message* (Fig. 3) elementary commercial exchange moment, which is closely correlated with each humanoid's emotional state and rational behavior (via "one-finger" on-off actions).

Introduction of Initial Assumptions

(1) Time interval θ is a random magnitude with $p(\theta)$ density that does not depend on t_j and u_j;

(2) Voltage drop (u_j) is a random magnitude with $p_1(u_j)$ density, which does not depend on t_j, and j; i.e , at the "switch-on" moment, the time of operation, or the quantity $R \equiv H$, switched on earlier (the Markovian process term);

Figure 3

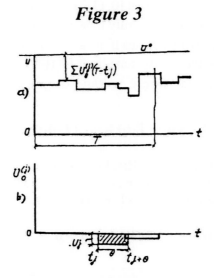

Fig. 3 V≡RB process stochastic formation
  a) function shaping;
  b) individual signal (on-off)

(3) $p_2(t_j)$ - density of probabilities at random moment t_j for the j-th connection, if it is known that this connection was within interval [O,T]. $p_2(t_j)$ does not depend on j.

(4) The probability of every R≡H connection during an infinitesimal interval is proportional to its active state intensity, $v(t)$:

$$P_1(dt) \equiv v(t)dt \qquad (8)$$

$v(t)$ - depends on social biorhythm intervals (night, day, etc.).

(5) The probability of more than one R ≡ H connection during an infinitesimal interval is even lower than dt:

$$P_{k>1}(dt) = O(dt), \qquad (9)$$

where

$O(dt)$ means that $\dfrac{O(dt)}{dt} \to 0$, when $dt \to 0$;

k – number of R≡H connected up.

(6) The probability of one R≡H connection does not depend on the quantity of R≡H, which are connected in another [O,T] interval.

This is approximately correct because a sample is finite.

If we accept the last three assumptions, the physical model shaped by the V≡RB stochastic process is described satisfactorily by the Poisson law for *flows with varying intensity*. The probability of k receivers' connection in the [O,T] interval is:

$$P_k(O,T) = \frac{\left[\int_0^T v(t)dt \right]^k}{k!} e^{-\int_0^T v(t)dt} \qquad (10)^{[19]}$$

---

[19] (1) Poisson law for flows with constant intensity $\left(P_k = \frac{(vt)^k}{k!} e^{-vt} \right)$ uses in the Ordered Queue theory.

(2) Assumptions (1 – 6) for the shaping of this model are true (**Appendix 2.2**).

$$U(T) = U^0 - \Sigma_j U_\theta^j (T-t_j) = U^0 - \tilde{U}(T) \qquad (11)$$

where

$\tilde{U}(T)$ – full voltage drop, caused by connection of k receivers before moment T.

The instantaneous density of probabilities should be defined. The instantaneous density for $U(T)$ for a stochastic process cycle of rational behavior (at **R≡H, GR≡GH, V≡RB**) thus will be defined as well. It is further demonstrated (**Appendix 2.3**) that the final expression of the desired density for moment **T** has the form:

$$p\left[\tilde{U}(T)\right] = -\frac{1}{\sqrt{2\pi}\sigma}\left[\varphi_0(x) - \frac{\alpha_3}{6\sigma^3}\varphi_1(x) - \frac{\alpha_4}{24\sigma^4}\varphi_2(x) + \right.$$

$$\left. +\frac{a_5}{120\sigma^5}\varphi_3(x) + \left(\frac{a_6}{120\sigma^6} + \frac{a_3^2}{72\sigma^6}\right)\varphi_4(x) + ...\right], \qquad (12)$$

where

$$\varphi_n(x) = (-1)^n \frac{d^n}{dx^n}e^{-\frac{x^2}{2}}; \qquad \left(x = \frac{\tilde{U}-\bar{U}}{\sigma}\right) \qquad (13)$$

$$\bar{U} = \bar{u}\theta * \frac{1}{T}\int_0^T v(t)dt; \qquad (14)$$

$$\sigma^2 = 2\theta * \int_0^T u^2 p_1(u)du \frac{1}{T}\int_0^T v(t)dt; \qquad (15)$$

$$\theta* = T\int_0^T p(\theta)d\theta \int_{T-\theta}^T p_2(t)dt \qquad (16)$$

34

The average value of the voltage drop as a result of the individual behavior, i.e., one receiver connection is:

$$\bar{u} = \int_0^\infty u p_1(u) du \qquad (17)$$

Factors a_n in the desired density (12) are equal to:

$$a_n = \theta * \frac{1}{T} \int_0^T v(t) dt \int_0^\infty u^n p_1(u) du, \qquad (18)$$
$$n = 3, 4, 5, \ldots$$

As can be seen from expression (12), the desired instantaneous density of the $V \equiv RB$ process probabilities is equal to the sum of normal distribution density and *additional units* which *distort* the Gaussian law.

It is also seen from (14) and (15) that the expression of density $p[\tilde{U}(T)]$ describes the non-stationary process because magnitudes π(mean) and σ (rms) depend on time. This dependence

is due to the existence of the multiple, $\theta * \frac{1}{T} \int_0^T v(t) dt$.

The form of series (12) allows us to conclude that the instantaneous fixed density of probabilities in the rational behavior cycle is close to the Gaussian distribution, if factors in the additional units $\varphi_n(x)$ are small. It is interesting to evaluate them quantitatively.

Let us evaluate factor $a_3/6\sigma^3$ at $\varphi_1(x)$. Using (15) and (18) with $n=3$, we will obtain

$$\frac{n_3}{6\sigma^3} = \frac{1}{12\sqrt{2}} \frac{\int\limits_0^\infty u^3 p_1(u)du}{\left[\int\limits_0^\infty u^2 p_1(u)du\right]^{3/2}} \frac{1}{\sqrt{\theta * \frac{1}{T}\int\limits_0^T v(t)dt}}. \qquad (19)$$

Factors in the higher-order units have the form $\dfrac{a_n}{\sigma^n}$ and $\dfrac{a_{n-i}a_i}{\sigma^n}$

They are established from the expressions:

$$\frac{a_n}{\sigma^n} = \frac{\int\limits_0^\infty u^n p_1(u)du}{\left[\int\limits_0^\infty u^2 p_1(u)du\right]^{n/2}\left[\theta * \frac{1}{T}\int\limits_0^T (v(t)dt\right]}; \qquad (20)$$

$$\frac{a_{n-i}a_i}{\sigma^n} = \frac{\int\limits_0^\infty u^{n-i}p_1(u)du\int\limits_0^\infty u^i p_1(u)du}{\left[\int\limits_0^\infty u^2 p_1(u)du\right]^{n/2}}\frac{1}{\left[\theta * \frac{1}{T}\int\limits_0^T v(t)dt\right]}; \qquad (21)$$

An analysis of (19) – (21) shows that the smaller the factors in units $\varphi_n(x)$, the greater the intensity of the $V\equiv RB$ process, i.e., the pace of the individual on-off process, and the average time of its operation dynamics.

2.4 3-D Linear-Discrete Model Construction

A sufficiently correct solution to both of the basic problems raised in 2.1 can be found through the experimental and theo-retical analysis performed in 2.2 and 2.3. This enables the creation of a formalized reliable model of rational behavior, i.e., the 24-hour model of the calendar-day social biorhythm.

This model is fully and adequately represented by the stochastic model of the AC service voltage function ($\pm$V tolerant deviations at reception) in urban electrical networks with one-phase receivers, the number of which is equal to the number of independent decisions **GR≡GH** (see 2.1).

Both models are shown graphically in Fig. 4. These models (**V** and **RB**) *are statistically fully identical*: during the 24-hour biorhythm cycle both models have absolutely identical $\tilde{M}(V) \equiv \tilde{M}(RB)$; sampled stationary probabilistic distribution where instantaneous density is close to the Gaussian curve. It is clear that the curves in the valid **V≡RB** function's mathematical expectation are a reciprocal mirror reflection, as can be seen in Fig. 4, but it should be emphasized that their statistical meanings are identical[20].

Based on this 3-D random, essentially non-stationary, model of 24-hour stochastic social biorhythm and its dynamic shaping, one can present some general conclusions. The correct method of analyzing the results of the measurements is evident from the presented pattern of the process. Statistical analysis must be performed for every stable recurrent (economic) stochastic signal, separately according to the segments of relative stationary revealed for each particular case.

---

[20] It should be emphasized that there is an essential difference in 3D space between physical (object coordinates) and economic (*time-utility-probability*) processes. Accordingly, the utility axis ($\pm$V) shapes two economic subspaces: "+" and "−" disutilities, with different economic content. For example, voltage ± tolerant rates have different economic meaning (damage). This anisotropic treatment of the specific features of economic space can be based, additionally, on N. Wiener's essay, "Newton and Bergson Time" [3].

Figure 4

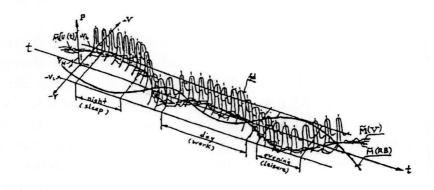

Fig. 4   Formalized 3-D stochastic V≡RB model for a stable
recurrent exchange process a calendar day.

$\tilde{M}$ –   mathematical expectation lines (thin
solid lines - individual realizations);

$\tilde{M}(V)$ –   AC mean phase voltage original
function at the delivery (thick dotted line);

$\tilde{M}(RB)$ –   rational behavior full-mirror function
(thick solid line);

$\pm V_L$ –   standard tolerant limits of each
individual signal (utility's instrumental
linear riterion);

fd   –   (fixed density) - distribution curves at
fixed moments (analytical result of App. 2.3);

T,V,P –   economic space axes (time-utility-probability).

The curve of the total distribution density for these separate relative stationary stochastic segments will be almost identical to the form of the instantaneous density curve, i.e., to the normal law curve (Gaussian approximation).

This approach to the statistical analysis of the $V \equiv RB$ model is illustrated by "plane" (not 3-D) construction (based on Fig. 4 and Appendix 2.1 numerical data), where, for fixed intervals of the process relative stationary (T_1, T_2 and T_3), through separate statistical analysis, three empirical histograms are constructed (Fig. 5). Clearly, all three histograms have one peak each; verification confirmed the high level of probabilistic convergence for each to empirical Gaussian distribution. This result unambiguously defines both the required amount of statistical information and the method by which it is obtained, which are needed to solve operational problems in applications (e.g., in *manufacturing process quality control with feedback data*).

The two simplest numerical characteristics that are obtained separately for each typical and stable mode during a 24-hour calendar cycle, mathematical expectation ($\bar{M}$) and root-mean-square deviation (σ), are most important. However, in most cases, mathematical expectation (mean) by intervals of process stationary is sufficient, as verified in Chapter 3 by economic assessment of utility for the canonic signal form: "valid signal" and centered function ("random noises").

Figure 5

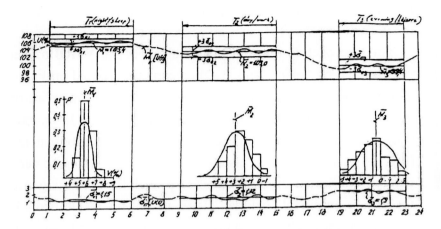

Fig. 5 Discrete presentation of 3D stochastic V=RB model as an essential time-dependent process with typical relative stationarity intervals (T_1, T_2, T_3). General form example.

General unified information (in the form of a bar-chart or single histogram), according to data from *the whole 24-hour day or multi-24-hour days* for non-stationary processes is applicable only for total probability assessment, i.e., for the establishment of fact. Because such a multi-24-hour histogram is the graphic form of the simplest variation series of changing parameters in several 24-hour cycles, different logical interpretations of its two numerical characteristics can appear very naive. Indeed, even the simplest questions, strictly speaking, are insoluble, if the 24-hour histogram (Fig. 6) does not contain any additional information (hatching and inscriptions: night, day, evening). A multi-day histogram does not provide objective information (partial probabilities) regarding to which time each stochastic process interval relates: to one or another subset of stable data or signal with one saddle point/local optimum [6]. The presence of two or more peaks on the 24-hour histogram (which is a reason for statements about the deviation from normal of the distribution law) is explained by the fact that such a histogram is essentially the result of averaging the process parameters by time of the sum total of all two-dimensional densities for fixed density (**fd**) moments in time (Fig. 4). The latter (two-dimensional densities) have one probability peak each, but these peaks can have different positions on the 24-hour time axis of the stochastic-social biorhythm/rational behavior model.

Thus, Chapter 2 constitutes the first part of the N-M classical problem solution (3-D Stochastic Linear-Discrete Model of **V≡RB** construction with four social saddle points). The second part is the subject of Chapter 3 (the 3D stochastic **V≡RB** model's probabilistic stability/feedback verification or axiomatic treatment of utility).

Figure 6

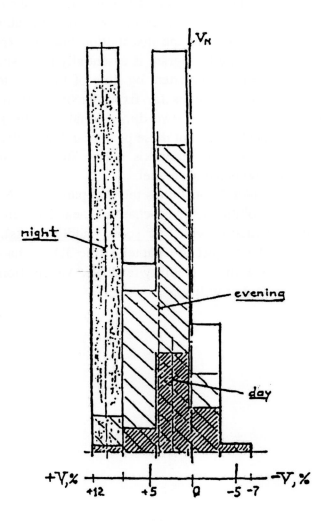

Fig. 6 **Typical experimental two-peak voltage histogram per calendar day in urban electrical networks with one-peak components on standard utility axis (±V, %): night, day, evening.**

Example of Stochastic Processing

As usual, it is difficult to examine the validity of the random process stationary hypothesis. Strictly, this must be carried out as a separate empirical study for each individual case and for each point of measurement. However, in this case cyclic recurrence of the $V \equiv RB$ function's factors and its similarity in each 24-hour cycle lead us to quite stable general conclusions on the basis of limited sample experimental results.

There is an instrumental record of AC service voltage stochastic function at delivery with time span sample 10-12 calendar days in running (on commercial electrical meter sockets).

(1) Minimal time of the continuous process record [19]:

$$T_{rec} \geq \frac{25}{\pi \cdot f_\ell} \geq 128 \text{ hrs} \qquad \text{(A2.1-1)}$$

where

$f_\ell = 1/t_\ell$ – the lowest frequency in the process. It corresponds to the longest period $T_{max} = 16$ hrs (accepted here for the $V \equiv RB$ curve). With $T_{rec} \geq 128$ hrs, the reliability of the correlation function is ensured by processing of no less than five 24-hour realizations recorded in day-to-day succession.

(2) Assume:

$$k_\ell = 2V, \, k_t - 1 \text{ hr}$$

(quantization of elementary intervals for level and time).

Verification of k, by quantization optimum for measured parameters (in this case, voltage):

$$K_\ell = \frac{x_{max} - x_{min}}{1 + 3,2\lg n} = 2.1v, \qquad (A2.1\text{-}2)$$

where

$x_{max} - x_{min}$ – variation scope of sampling,

$n = 720$ – number of quantized sampling probes. Optimum verification of k_t according to the Naiquist – Kotelnikov formula:

$$k_t = 1/(2f_h) = 1 \text{ hr} \qquad (A2.1\text{-}3)$$

where

$f_h = 1/T_h$ – the highest frequency. It corresponds to the shortest period T=2 hr (accepted for the V≡RB curve). Taking into account the low frequency spectrum of V≡RB stochastic components, this value of k_t is quite acceptable.

As applied to the correlation function, the biggest stochastic scale is equal:

$$\tau_{max} \geq (0.1\text{-}0.2)T_{rec} \geq 12 + 13 \text{ hr} \qquad (A2.1\text{-}4)$$

with $\tau_{min} = k = 1$ hr (minimal stochastic lag) for the V≡RB correlation function.

(3) Calculation of V≡RB numerical parameters by

a) Chebyshev's "Method of Moments," where $\tilde{M}(t)$, $\overset{\circ}{\sigma}(t)$ are current values (see Table 1) and

b) Construction of the correlation matrices R(τ).

Normalization is based on the expression for the continuous processes:

$$R_{x,y}(t_i,...,t_j) = \int_{-\infty}^{\infty} \int_{-\infty}^{\infty} \overset{\circ}{x}\overset{\circ}{y} \, p(x,t_i)p(y,t_j)dxdy \qquad (A2.1\text{-}5)$$

Since this function includes one argument, the operation of quantization makes is possible to go over to discrete values. The following expression is sued for the autocorrelative moments:

$$R(t_i,...,t_j) = \sum_{i=1}^{s} \sum_{j=1}^{r} \overset{\circ}{x} x_j p(x_i t_j, x_j t_i) \qquad (A2.1\text{-}6)$$

44

or $\qquad$ $R(\tau) = M\overset{\circ}{x}(t_i)\overset{\circ}{x}(t_j),$ $\qquad$ (A2.1-7)

where

$\overset{\circ}{x}$ – current values of the centered function in the section

t_i or $t_j = t_i + \tau$.

Elements in the normalized matrix correlation field or correlation ratio $\overline{\rho}\,(\tau)$ for 24 sections (according to the number of quantization intervals) are drawn from the normalization condition

$$\overline{e}(\tau) = \frac{R(\tau)}{\sigma(t_i)\sigma(t_j)} \qquad (A2.1-8)$$

where

$\sigma(t_i)$ and $\sigma(t_j)$ conform to the values of the correlated sections.

The computed calculated correlation matrices – natural and normalized – are given here (see Table A2.2 – 2.3).

An analysis of both Table 1 (method of moments) and the correlation matrices shows that statistical units of the process in the identical sections are quite close to one another. It indicates reliability of the given statistical processing. As can be seen, all numerical characteristics vary in their value, and the sub-up-diagonal sections of the correlation matrices are also not uniform. These signs suggest a hypothesis of the time-dependent function. A qualitative analysis of the results is given in Chapter 2.

(4) M,D,σ assessment according to the error theory

(a) Sliding average:

$$\tilde{M}(t) = \frac{1}{2\ell \cdot n} \sum_{a=1}^{n} \sum_{i=j-\ell}^{i=j+\ell} u_a(t_i) \qquad (A2.1-9)$$

(b) Assessment of $\tilde{M}(t)$ is calculated by realizations after which it is smoothed by the sliding average method (on three valid meanings).

45

Then

$$\tilde{m}^* = \frac{\sum\limits_{j}^{j=3} \bar{M}(t_j)}{3} \qquad \text{(A2.1-10)}$$

(c) Assessment of m is averaged in relative stationary interval T:

$$m^* = M(t) = \frac{1}{T} \sum_{i=1}^{\ell} \tilde{m}_i = \overline{\overline{M}}_T \qquad \text{(A2.1-11)}$$

where

thick line over M(t) – averaging by time;

thin line over M(t) – averaging by set;

(d) Averaged unbiased assessment of variance:

$$D_0(m^*) = \frac{\tilde{D}(t)}{\ell - 1} \equiv \frac{\dfrac{1}{2\ell n} \sum\limits_{\alpha=1}^{n} \sum\limits_{\ell=1}^{\ell} [U_a(t_j) - M_T]^2}{\ell - 1} \qquad \text{(A2.1-12)}$$

$\overline{\sigma}_{OT} = \dfrac{\overline{\sigma}}{\sqrt{\ell n}}$, where ℓn = number of independent measurement probes.

(e) Variance of the variability measure:

$$\tilde{D}(D_T^*) = \frac{2}{\ell k_t - 1}(\overline{D})^2 \qquad \text{(A2.1-13)}$$

D_T^* is of unbiased assessment.

Its averaged variation:

$$\overline{D}(D_T^*) = \frac{\tilde{D}[(D_T^*)]}{\ell} \qquad \text{(A2.1-14)}$$

$$\overline{\sigma}(D_T^*) = \frac{\overline{\sigma}[(D_T^*)]}{\sqrt{2\ell n}} \qquad \text{(A2.1-15)}$$

(f) Results of calculations (5) are recorded in Table (A2-1):

Table A2-1

Assessment	T_1	T_2	T_3
M_T , %	101.4	103.7	101.9
$D_T[\tilde{m}]$,%^{2}	0.92	1.15	1.7
$\bar{\sigma}_T[\tilde{m}]$,%	0.19	0.18	0.26
$\bar{D}[D_T]$,%^{2}	0.08	0.12	0.29
$\bar{\sigma}_0$,%$[D_T]$,%	0.02	0.05	0.10

The values given in Table A2.1-1 are represented in the form of inequalities (3, 4, 5); they confirmed our hypothesis of the $V \equiv RB$ function's
essential non-stationary (time-dependent) character.

Correlation Matrices of V RB (24-hour behavioristic cycle)

Table A2. 1-2
Natural Correlation matrix

t_j \ t_i	0-1	1-2	2-3	3-4	4-5	5-6	6-7	7-8	8-9	9-10	10-11	11-12
0-1	0.87	0.77	0.75	0.74	0.59	0.44	-0.12	-0.27	-0.41	-0.32	-0.29	0.19
1-2		0.91	0.81	0.75	0.67	-0.51	0.30	0.24	0.13	0.12	0.09	0.08
2-3			1.11	0.77	0.68	0.48	0.36	0.28	0.16	0.14	0.14	0.12
3-4				0.94	0.79	0.57	-0.32	0.35	0.18	0.15	0.15	0.13
4-5					0.91	0.84	0.41	0.37	0.19	0.17	0.20	-0.16
5-6						1.92	0.81	1.06	-0.59	0.23	0.22	0.18
6-7							0.41	0.37	0.34	0.28	0.25	0.18
7-8								1.42	-0.14	0.87	0.62	-0.11
8-9									0.91	0.70	0.64	0.38
9-10										0.21	0.91	0.48
10-11											1.03	0.76
11-12												0.88
12-13												0.97
13-14												
14-15												
15-16												
16-18												
17-19												
18-19												
19-20												
20-21												
21-22												
22-23												
23-24												

Correlation Matrices of V RB (24-hour behavioristic cycle)

Table A2. 1-2 (cont.)

Natural Correlation matrix

t	12-13	13-14	14-15	15-16	16-17	17-18	18-19	19-20	20-21	21-22	22-23	23-24
0-1	0.14	-0.77	0.10	0.10	0.09	-0.21	-0.01	0.04	-0.08	-0.11	-0.02	-0.01
1-2	-0.16	0.11	-0.17	0.16	0.01	0.10	-0.08	-0.11	0.09	0.07	0.06	-0.02
2-3	0.12	0.13	0.18	0.13	-0.18	0.11	0.08	0.07	-0.07	-0.13	0.08	0.03
3-4	0.12	-0.31	0.12	0.10	0.10	-0.15	-0.04	0.09	0.09	0.08	0.08	0.03
4-5	-0.13	0.12	0.12	0.11	0.11	0.09	0.10	-0.10	-0.12	0.13	0.10	-0.04
5-6	0.18	0.14	-0.28	-0.13	0.12	0.11	0.10	0.10	-0.13	-0.21	-0.09	0.06
6-7	-0.07	0.22	0.17	0.17	0.14	-0.03	-0.12	0.08	0.12	0.10	0.10	0.08
7-8	0.35	0.34	0.20	-0.12	-0.09	0.16	0.14	-0.19	0.11	-0.08	0.10	0.10
8-9	0.40	0.36	0.21	0.17	0.18	-0.04	0.16	0.13	-0.11	0.08	0.10	-0.09
9-10	0.61	0.61	0.49	0.46	-0.13	0.23	0.19	0.16	0.15	0.13	0.11	0.10
10-11	0.80	0.71	0.63	0.54	0.29	0.21	-0.14	0.19	0.17	-0.07	0.16	0.11
11-12	0.81	0.74	0.64	0.60	0.33	-0.20	0.13	0.13	-0.10	0.19	-0.08	0.14
12-13	0.95	0.84	0.81	0.67	0.44	0.27	0.14	0.14	0.10	-0.08	0.18	0.15
13-14		1.04	0.90	0.75	0.50	0.43	0.37	0.29	-0.12	0.28	-0.14	0.21
14-15			1.06	0.86	0.62	-0.82	0.54	10.43	0.41	-0.07	0.11	-0.23
15-16				1.02	0.81	1.24	0.76	-0.	-0.11	0.22	0.15	-0.16
16-17					0.75	1.16	0.83	0.39	0.37	0.36	0.31	0.29
17-18						2.02	0.94	0.91	0.65	-0.41	0.44	0.27
18-19							1.69	1.38	1.27	1.23	0.96	0.31
19-20								1.42	1.26	0.98	1.16	0.37
20-21									1.48	1.28	1.15	-0.21
21-22										1.59	1.44	0.34
22-23											1.71	0.11
23-24												0.27

Correlation Matrices of V RB (24-hour behavioristic cycle)

Table A2. 1-3
Normalized Correlation matrix

t	0-1	1-2	2-3	3-4	4-5	5-6	6-7	7-8	8-9	9-10	10-11	11-12
0-1	1	0.87	0.82	0.78	0.67	0.34	-0.22	-0.24	-0.46	-0.32	-0.33	0.21
1-2		1	0.84	0.81	0.75	-0.39	0.50	0.21	0.15	0.12	0.10	0.09
2-3			1	0.75	0.68	0.45	0.33	0.23	0.16	0.12	0.12	0.11
3-4				1	0.86	0.42	-0.41	0.27	0.19	0.13	0.15	0.14
4-5					1	0.67	0.63	0.32	0.21	0.16	0.20	-0.14
5-6						1	0.91	0.64	-0.45	0.16	0.15	0.13
6-7							1	0.56	0.48	0.4	0.38	-0.17
7-8								1	-0.12	0.67	0.51	0.32
8-9									1	0.68	0.67	0.52
9-10										1	0.82	0.70
10-11											1	0.88
11-12												1
12-13												
13-14												
14-15												
15-16												
16-18												
17-19												
18-19												
19-20												
20-21												
21-22												
22-23												
23-24												

Correlation Matrices of V RB (24-hour behavioristic cycle)

Table A2. 1-3 (cont.)

Normalized Correlation matrix

t / t	12-13	13-14	14-15	15-16	16-17	17-18	18-19	19-20	20-21	21-22	22-23	23-24
0-1	0.15	-0.10	0.11	0.10	0.11	-0.12	-0.01	0.03	-0.07	-0.09	-0.02	0.03
1-2	-0.18	0.12	0.08	0.17	0.02	0.06	-0.07	-0.09	0.07	0.05	0.04	-0.01
2-3	0.12	0.11	0.16	0.13	-0.19	0.07	0.06	0.05	-0.05	-0.10	0.04	0.06
3-4	0.13	-0.32	0.12	0.11	0.12	-0.11	-0.03	0.08	0.07	0.07	0.06	0.06
4-5	-0.17	0.13	0.13	0.11	0.12	0.07	0.08	-0.16	-0.10	-0.11	0.08	-0.07
5-6	0.13	0.10	-0.21	-0.11	0.10	0.06	0.05	0.06	-0.07	-0.12	-0.08	0.08
6-7	-0.11	0.34	0.26	0.26	0.11	0.04	-0.15	0.1	0.15	0.07	0.12	0.25
7-8	0.3	0.28	0.17	0.10	-0.09	0.10	0.09	-0.07	0.08	-0.05	0.06	0.16
8-9	0.43	0.40	0.22	0.19	0.22	-0.03	0.13	0.11	-0.1	0.07	0.08	-0.18
9-10	0.55	0.53	0.43	0.42	-0.14	0.13	0.13	0.12	0.11	0.09	0.07	0.19
10-11	0.83	0.71	0.59	0.53	0.34	0.15	-0.11	0.1	0.14	-0.04	0.12	0.21
11-12	0.85	0.75	0.64	0.61	0.39	-0.14	0.10	0.11	-0.08	0.15	-0.06	-0.28
12-13	1	0.88	0.82	0.68	0.52	0.21	0.11	0.12	0.08	-0.06	0.14	0.31
13-14		1	0.89	0.74	0.58	0.32	0.28	0.24	-0.10	0.22	-0.11	0.42
14-15			1	0.86	0.69	-0.57	0.42	0.36	0.32	-0.05	0.08	-0.81
15-16				1	0.94	0.85	0.57	-0.15	-0.09	0.17	0.11	-0.31
16-17					1	0.93	0.73	0.39	0.37	0.33	0.27	0.21
17-18						1	0.51	0.53	0.38	-0.24	0.23	0.38
18-19							1					
19-20							0.9	1				
20-21							0.81	0.87	1			
21-22							0.75	0.65	0.85	1		
22-23							0.56	0.71	0.71	0.84	1	
23-24							0.46	0.58	-0.34	0.51	0.17	1

Integral Poisson Law Identity

According to the initial assumption 6 (§2.3):

$$P_k(T+dt) = P_{k-1}(T) \cdot P_1(P_1(dt) + P_k(T) \cdot P_0(dt)$$

but P_1 (dt) = v(T)d ⚡ (assumption 4)   (A2.2-1)

Therefore,

$$P_k(T+dt) = P_{k-1}(T) \cdot v(T)dt + P_k(T)-$$

$$P_k(T+)v(T)dt - P_k(T) \cdot O (dt)$$ (A2.2-2)

Dividing (A2.2-2) by dt and transforming it:

$$\frac{P_k(T+dt) - P_k(T)}{dt} = v(T[P_{k-1}(T) - P_k(T)] - \frac{P_k(T) \cdot O(dt)}{dt}$$ (A2.2-3)

or getting to limit, (assumption 5)

$$P_k'(T) = v(T)[P_{k-1}(T) - P_k(T)]$$ (A2.2-4)

Now, we need to be convinced that probability $P_k(T)$ satisfies equation (A.2.2-4). Taking derivation (10), we get

$$P_k'(T) = \frac{\left[\int_0^T v(T)dt\right]^{k-1} v(T)}{(k-1)!} e^{-\int_0^T v(T)dt} - \frac{\left[\int_0^T v(T)dt\right]^k v(T)}{k!} e^{-\int_0^T v(T)dt}$$

$$= v(T)P_{k-1}(T) - v(T)P_k(T) = v(T)[P_{k-1}(T) - P_k(T)]$$ (A.2.2-5)

One can see, that the substitution (A2.2-5) turns (A2.2-4) into an identity, that corroborates Poisson Law's adequate approximation for V≡RB stochastic process, correct probabilistic shaping.

52

Instantaneous Density Analysis

Let $\tilde{U}$ (T) be the voltage drop caused by all receivers switched on before moment T, i.e.,

$$\tilde{U}(T) = \sum_j u_\theta^{(j)}(T - t_j) \qquad \text{(A2.3-1)}$$

where $u_\theta^{(j)}$ (T-t) has form (11).

Let us consider the characteristic function (the ch.f.) of the random value $\tilde{U}$ (T):

$$\Phi_{\tilde{u}}(\lambda) = M[e^{j\tilde{u}}], \qquad \text{(A2.3-2)}$$

where λ is a real argument of the ch.f.

Let us introduce random quantity $\tilde{u}_K$:

$$\tilde{u}_k = \sum_{j=1}^{k} u_\theta^{(j)}(T - j_j) \quad (-0,1,2,...) . \qquad \text{(A2.3-3)}$$

where $\tilde{u}_K$ is a voltage drop in the interval [O,T] provided the number of k receivers is ultimate (R ≡ H).

Random value $\tilde{u}$ (T) thus assumes values of $\tilde{u}_K$ with $p_K(T)$ probabilities. Hence, the ch.f. for $\tilde{U}$ (T):

$$\Phi_{\tilde{u}}(\lambda) = \sum_{k=0}^{\infty} p_k(T)M[e^{i\lambda\tilde{u}_k}] = \sum_{k=0}^{\infty} p_k(T)\Phi_{\tilde{U}_k}(\lambda) \qquad \text{(A2.3-4)}$$

where $\Phi_{\tilde{u}}(\lambda)$ is the ch.f. of random value quantity $\tilde{U}_K$ [1].

---

[1] The ch.f. method ($\Phi_{\tilde{u}}(\lambda)$) (definition is based on Fourier's transform couple [M[$e^{i\lambda}$ $\tilde{u}^k$] and $\Phi_{\tilde{u}}(\lambda)$). As to full convergence, the ch.f. method is simpler than the direct [M[$e^{i\lambda}$ $\tilde{u}^k$] density model construction. This is the core of S. Rice's well-known interpretation, which is also used here [4].

If k = 0 (all receivers are disconnected), then $\tilde{U}_0 = 0$. For the ch.f. of random value $\tilde{U}_K$:

$$\Phi\hat{U}_o(\lambda)M[e^0] = 1.$$ (A2.3-5)

If k ≥1, then:

$$\Phi\tilde{U}_1(\lambda) = M[e^{i\lambda\tilde{U}_\lambda}] = M\left[e^{i\lambda\sum_{j=1}^{k}u_\theta(j)T-t_j)}\right] =$$

$$= M[\sum_{j=1}^{k} e^{i\lambda u_\theta(j)(T-t_j)}] = \sum_{j=1}^{k} M\left[e^{i\lambda\sum_{j=1}^{k}u_\theta(j)T-t_j)}\right] =$$

$$= \left\{M[e^{i\lambda u_\theta(j)(T-t)}]\right\}^k = \left[\Phi\tilde{U}_k(\lambda)\right]^k ,$$ (A2.3-6)

where

$$\Phi\tilde{U}_k(\lambda) = U_\theta(T\text{-}t).$$ (A2.3-7)

The mutual dependence of elementary individual decisions and the voltage drops caused by them were used to derive (A2.3-7), i.e., $U_\theta(T-t_j)$ with j = 1,2,... as independent random values. Hence, the ch.f., by the sum of these values, is equal to ch.f. for separate terms.

In (A2.3-7) and in the last part of expression (A2.3-6), the subscript j is omitted, because all probabilities/densities, as indicated before, do not depend on the value and number j. Hence, the ch.f. of all factors (A2.3-6) are the same values.

Then, taking into account (A2.3-6), the following is obtained:

54

$$\Phi\tilde{U}_k\ (\lambda) = M\left[e^{i\lambda u_{\bullet}(j)(T-t_j)}\right] = \int\limits_0^\infty p_1(u)du\int\limits_0^\infty p(\theta)d\theta\int\limits_0^\infty p_2(t)\times$$

$$\times\ e^{(\lambda\{uE(T-t)-uE(T-\theta-t\}}dt = \int\limits_0^\infty p_1(u)du\ \int\limits_0^\infty p(\theta)d\theta\times$$

$$\times\left[\int\limits_0^T p_2(t)e^{i\lambda u}dt + \int\limits_0^{T-\theta} p_2(t)dt\right]+$$

$$+\int\limits_0^\infty p_1(u)du\ \int\limits_T^\infty p(\theta)d\theta\int\limits_0^T p_2(t)e^{i\lambda u}dt \ . \tag{A2.3-8}$$

The last term of expression (A2.3-8) can be set to be equal to zero since interval [O,T] is of long duration (the moments which are remote from the initial one are considered), and the probability that $\theta>T$ is very low. Therefore, in the [O,T] boundaries, density $\int\limits_0^\infty p(\theta)d\theta$ is also negligible. Factoring $e^{i\lambda u}$ outside the integrals over t and θ signs, we obtain

$$\Phi\tilde{U}_1\ (\lambda) = \int\limits_0^\infty e^{i\lambda u}p_1(u)du\int\limits_0^T p(\theta)d\theta\ \int\limits_{T-\theta}^T p_2(t)dt +$$

$$+\int\limits_0^\infty p_1(u)du\ \int\limits_0^T p(\theta)d\theta\times\ \int\limits_0^{T-\theta} p_2(t)dt =$$

$$=\int\limits_0^\infty e^{i\lambda u}p_1(u)du\int\limits_0^T p(\theta)d\theta\ \int\limits_{T-\theta}^T p_2(t)dt +$$

$$+\int\limits_0^T p(\theta)d\theta\int\limits_0^T p_2(t)dt -\int\limits_0^T p(\theta)d\theta\ \int\limits_{T-\theta}^T p_2(t)dt =$$

$$=\ \int\limits_0^\infty e^{i\lambda u}p_1(u)du \cdot a + 1 - a\ , \tag{A2.3-9}$$

where

$$a = \int_0^T p(\theta)d\theta \int_{T-\theta}^T p_2(t)dt \qquad \text{(A2.3-10)}^2$$

For instance, if intensity $v(t)$ is constant, then $p_2(t) = 1/T$; the receivers' operation has equal probabilities for all moments t within [O,T]. Then:

$$a = \int_0^T p(\theta)d\theta \frac{1}{t}\int_{T-\theta}^T dt = \frac{1}{T}\int_0^T \textbf{p}\,(\theta)d\theta = \frac{\overline{\theta}}{T}, \qquad \text{(A2.3-11)}$$

where $\overline{\theta}$ is the average duration of each receiver operation.

In general,

$$\Phi\tilde{U}_1\,(\lambda) = \left[\int_0^\infty p_1(u)e^{i\lambda u}du\right] + 1. \qquad \text{(A2.3-12)}$$

Defining the average of U :

$$M[\tilde{u}] = \sum_{k=0}^\infty p_k(T)M[\tilde{u}_k]. \qquad \text{(A2.3-13)}$$

From (A2.3-6) it follows that $\Phi_{k\geq1}(\lambda) = [\Phi_{k\geq1}(\lambda)]^k$. Then, according to the theorem on the derivation of the ch.f.:

$$M[\tilde{U}_k] = \frac{\Phi'U_k^{(0)}}{i}\frac{k[\Phi'U_1^{(0)}]^{k-1}\Phi'U_1^{(0)}]}{i} = k\Phi'U_1^{(0)} =$$

$$= ka\int_0^\infty up_1(u)du = ka\overline{u}, \qquad \text{(A2.3-14)}$$

where $\overline{u} = \int_0^\infty up_1(u)du$ is the average voltage drop after one receiver is switched on.

Let us find average $\overline{U}$, using (A2.3-14):

---

[2] Taken into consideration here was the case where $\int_0^\infty p_1(u)du = 1$ (normalizing condition.)

$$\bar{U} = M[\tilde{u}[= \sum_{k=0}^{\infty} p_k(T)ka\bar{u} = a\bar{u}\sum_{k=0}^{\infty} \frac{k\left[\int_0^T v(t)dt\right]^k e^{-\int_0^T v(t)dt}}{k!} =$$

$$=a\bar{u}e^{-\int_0^T v(t)dt}\int_0^T v(t)dt\sum_{k=1}^{\infty} \frac{(k-1)\left[\int_0^T v(t)dt\right]^{k-1}}{(k-1)!} = a\bar{u}\int_0^T v(t)dt. \qquad (A2.3\text{-}15)$$

If intensity $v(t) = $ const., then using (A2.3-11) we obtain:

$$\bar{U} = \frac{\bar{\theta}}{T}\bar{u}vT = \bar{u}\bar{\theta}v \qquad (A2.3\text{-}16)$$

Now, let us define the ch.f. for $\tilde{U}$, keeping in mind that $\tilde{U}$ with probability $P_K(T)$ is equal to the random value, $\tilde{U}_K$ $(k = 0,1,2,...)$. Therefore:

$$\Phi_{\tilde{U}}(\lambda) = \sum_{k=0}^{\infty} p_k(T)\Phi_{\tilde{U}_k}(\lambda) = \sum_{k=0}^{\infty} p_k(T)[\Phi\tilde{U}_1(\lambda)]^k =$$

$$= \sum_{k=0}^{\infty} \frac{k\left[\int_0^T v(t)dt\right]^k}{k!}e^{-\int_0^T v(t)dt}[\Phi\tilde{U}_1(\lambda)]^k =$$

$$= e^{-\int_0^T v(t)dt}\exp\left\{\int v(t)dt\Phi_{\tilde{U}_1}(\lambda)\right\}. \qquad (A2.3\text{-}17)$$

Substituting (A2.3-12) for (A2.3-17) we obtain

$$\Phi_{\tilde{U}_1}(\lambda) = \exp\left\{a\int_0^T v(t)dt\left[\int_0^\infty p_1(u)e^{i\lambda u}du - 1\right]\right\}. \qquad \text{(A2.3-18)}$$

Let us expand the exponent of the function power in (A2.3-18) in a series by powers of u:

$$\Phi_{\tilde{U}}(\lambda) = \exp\ i\lambda a\int_0^T v(t)dt\int_0^\infty p_1(u)udu -$$

$$- \lambda^2 a\int_0^T v(t)dt\int_0^\infty u^2 p_1(u)udu +$$

$$+ a\int_0^T v(t)dt\sum_{n=3}^\infty \frac{(i\lambda)^n}{n!}\int_0^\infty u^n p_1(u)udu =$$

$$= \exp\left\{i\lambda\bar{U} - \frac{\lambda^2\sigma^2}{2}\right\}\exp\left\{a\int_0^T v(t)dt\sum_{n=3}^\infty \frac{(i\lambda)^n}{n!}\int_0^\infty u^n p_1(u)du\right\}, \qquad \text{(A2.3-19)}$$

where $\bar{U}$ is derived from (A2.3-15).

Let us denote

$$\sigma^2 = 2a\int_0^T v(t)dt\int_0^\infty u^n p_1(u)du \qquad \text{(A2.3-20)}$$

and

$$a\int_0^T v(t)dt\int_0^\infty u^n p_1(u)du = a_n, \qquad \text{(A2.3-21)}$$

where $a_1 = U$; $a_2 = \dfrac{\sigma_0}{2}$.

After re-writing (A2.3-19), and taking (A2.3-21), we obtain

$$\Phi_{\tilde{U}}(\lambda) = \exp\left\{i\lambda\bar{U} - \frac{\lambda^2\sigma^2}{2}\right\}\exp\left\{\sum_{n=3}^\infty \frac{(i\lambda)^n}{n!}a_n +\right.$$

58

$$+ \frac{1}{2!}\left[\sum_{n=3}^{\infty} \frac{(i\lambda)^n}{n!}a_n\right]^2 + \frac{1}{3!}\left[\sum_{n=3}^{\infty} \frac{(i\lambda)^n}{n!}a_n\right]^3 + ...\Bigg\} =$$

$$= \exp\left\{i\lambda\tilde{U} - \frac{\lambda^2\sigma^2}{2}\right\}\exp\left\{\sum_{n=3}^{\infty} \frac{a_n(i\lambda)^n}{n!}\right\}. \qquad (A2.3\text{-}22)$$

Let us express the desired density of probabilities through its ch.f.

$$p(\tilde{U}) = \frac{1}{2\pi}\int_{-\infty}^{\infty} e^{i\lambda\tilde{U}}\Phi_{\tilde{U}}(\lambda)d\lambda. \qquad (A2.3\text{-}23)$$

We now expand an expression into a series for the possibility of ch.f. (A2.3-23) integration:

$$\exp\left\{\sum_{n=3}^{\infty} a_n \frac{(i\lambda)^n}{n!}\right\} \qquad (A2.3\text{-}24)$$

limiting ourselves to finding several series units:

$$\exp\left\{\sum_{n=3}^{\infty} a_n \frac{(i\lambda)^n}{n!}\right\} = 1 + a_3 \frac{(i\lambda)^3}{3!} + a_4 \frac{(i\lambda)^4}{4!} +$$

$$+ a5 \frac{(i\lambda)^5}{5!} + (i\lambda)^6\left[\frac{a_6}{6!} + \frac{1}{2!}\frac{a_3^2}{(3!)^2}\right]... \qquad (A2.3\text{-}25)$$

(A2.3-22) is now rewritten in the following form, taking (A2.3-25) into account:

$$\Phi_{\tilde{U}}(\lambda) = \exp\left\{i\lambda\tilde{U} - \frac{\lambda^2\sigma^2}{2}\right\}\left[1 + \frac{a_3(i\lambda)^3}{3!} + \right.$$

$$\left. + \frac{a_4(i\lambda)^4}{4!} + \frac{a_5(i\lambda)^5}{5!} + \dots\right] \tag{A2.3-26}$$

Returning to expression (A2.3-25) and using (A2.3-25) and (A2.3-26), we proceed from the ch.f. to the desired density of probabilities:

$$p(\tilde{u}) = \frac{1}{2\pi}\int_{-}^{-} \exp\left\{i\lambda(\tilde{U}-\bar{U}) - \frac{\lambda^2\sigma^2}{2}\right\}\left\{1 + \frac{a_3(i\lambda)^3}{3!} + \frac{a_4(i\lambda)^4}{4!} + \right.$$

$$\left. + \frac{a_5(i\lambda)^5}{5!} + (i\lambda)^6\left[\frac{a_6}{6!} + \frac{a_3^2}{2!(3!)^2}\right] + \dots\right\}d\lambda. \tag{A2.3-27}$$

The normalized random value is now introduced :

$$x = \frac{\tilde{U}-\bar{U}}{\sigma} \tag{A2.3-28}$$

Then, going in (A2.3-27) to the term-by-term integration, we obtain:

$$p(\tilde{u}) = \frac{1}{2\pi}\int_{-}^{-} \exp\left(i\lambda\sigma x - \frac{\lambda^2\sigma^2}{2}\right)d\lambda +$$

$$+ \frac{1}{2\pi}\frac{a_3}{3!\sigma^2}\int_{-}^{-}(i\lambda\sigma)^2\exp\left(i\lambda(\sigma x - \frac{\lambda^2\sigma^2}{2}\right)d\lambda +$$

$$+ \frac{a_5(i\lambda)^5}{5!} + (i\lambda)^6\left[\frac{a_6}{6!} + \frac{a_3^2}{2!(3!)^2}\right] + \dots\right\}d\lambda. \tag{A2.3-29}$$

Let us consider the integral:

$$I_n(x) = \frac{1}{2\pi}\int_{-}^{-}\exp\left(i\lambda\sigma x - \frac{\lambda^2\sigma^2}{2}\right)d\lambda \qquad\text{(A2.3-30)}$$

$$(n=0,1,2,...)$$

According to [4]:

$$I_0(x) = \frac{1}{2\pi}\int_{0}^{-}e^{-i\lambda\sigma x -\frac{\lambda^2\sigma^2}{2}}d\lambda = \frac{1}{\sqrt{2\pi}\sigma}e^{-\frac{x^2}{2}} \qquad\text{(A2.3-31)}$$

and

$$I_n(x) = (-1)^n\frac{d^nI_0(x)}{dx^n} = \frac{(-1)^nd^n}{a\sqrt{2\pi}dx}e^{-\frac{x^2}{2}} \qquad\text{(A2.3-32)}$$

Let us denote:

$$\varphi_0(x) = e^{-\frac{x^2}{2}}; \qquad\text{(A2.3-33)}$$

$$\varphi_n(x) = (-1)^n\frac{d^n}{dx^n}e^{-\frac{x^2}{2}} \qquad\text{(A2.3-34)}$$

The desired density of probabilities, written in final form is:

$$p[\tilde{U}(T)] = \frac{1}{\sqrt{2\pi}\sigma}\left[\varphi_0(x) - \frac{a_3}{6\sigma^3}\varphi_1(x) + \frac{a_4}{24\sigma^4}\varphi_2(x) + \right.$$
$$\left. +\frac{a_5}{120\sigma^5}\varphi_3(x) + \left(\frac{a_6}{120\sigma^6} + \frac{a_3^2}{72\sigma^6}\right)\varphi_4(x) + ...\right]. \qquad\text{(A2.3-35)}[3]$$

---

[3] This convergent power series (A2.3-35) presents *the analytical solution of a second basic problem* (see 2.1). Its graphical form is presented in the general 3-D stochastic V≡RB model as a fixed instantaneous density (Fig. 4): **fd.**

CHAPTER 3

Standard Probability of V≡RB Model Utility

**Our axioms make utility a number –
up to a linear transformation.**

J. von Neumann, O. Morgenstern, 1944

**The process by which we resist the
corruption and decay is homeostasis
(feedback).**

N. Wiener, 1947

3.1 The Notion of Disutility

One of the original facets of the Voltage Paradox is
P. Ailleret's pioneering idea that the AC service voltage
functional quality due to electrical receivers' operation is
proportional to *the mean square of voltage random fluctuations* during an assumed time interval [5]. According to Ailleret, voltage instability (*disutility*) D is:

$$\mathbf{D_v} = \frac{1}{\mathbf{T}} \int_0^{\mathbf{T}} \mathbf{V^2 dt} \qquad (22)^1$$

This approach, being a fundamental base for random AC
voltage treatment, was virtually unnoticed, except by a few
electrical engineers in Europe (some statistical instruments
were invented for $\mathbf{D_v}$ measurement). This was caused by a
general misunderstanding of the true meaning of the $\mathbf{D_v}$ "exotic" rate in econometrics as the only statistical tool for the
valid analysis of economic utility (including the author of this
study, 25 years ago). Only J. Chervonenkis [19] in 1965 sug-

---

[1] Time is the only argument of this trivial, but fundamental criterion.

gested a new, nonobvious hypothesis based on this notion: The full empirical, tolerant AC service voltage ratings at delivery ($\pm$ 5%, $\pm$6%, etc.) are statistical-economic norms; *they relate to voltage mathematical expectation.* The general correctness of this "local" (electrical) statement is proved here by use of the general meaning of the voltage paradox and the 3D stochastic $\mathbf{V \equiv RB}$ model (Chapters 1, 2). The following should be noted:

(1) Because the disutility function $\mathbf{D_v}$ is as continuous as is voltage $\mathbf{V(t)}$ and has derivations on each stochastic interval, the possibility of expanding it into the Taylor series is not subject to debate;

(2) The unknown form of the disutility function, $\mathbf{D_v}$, for one receiver ($\mathbf{R \equiv H}$) or group ($\mathbf{GR \equiv GH}$) does not allow for strict quantitative estimation as to the finite error by the Lagrange – Koshi reminder for the Taylor series (which is limited by the second order unit). The vicinity of typical tolerant steady-state limits (e.g., $\mathbf{V_N = \pm 5\%}$), however, can be considered sufficiently small for the claim that the disutility function D_v can be approximated here as *the second order* polynomial.

As expected, the numerous instrumental investigations of this empirical assumption for many electrical receivers (light bulb, AC motor, etc.) merely confirmed the fundamental meaning of the second order notion.

The subject matter is that *squareness has the deepest philosophical sense; it is a standard for the stochastic interactivity of "matter-energy" in Nature*; it is a standard form of power for virtually all stable recurrent processes with functional and statistical correlation. This is true for nuclear energy, power technology, and mechanics, as well as for statistics. All the great physical-mathematical notions (Newtonian, Lagrangian, Hamiltonian metrics, Lebesque measure) are in the quadratic form. The basic calculus of the variations thesis is: *extremals of the convex functions set are, in essence, quadratic parabolas.* All optimization procedures in applications are based on this formulation. The *squareness principle* runs through classic and relativistic physics, from Galileo to Einstein. It is the only key to the crucial role of *mathematical expectation* (mean) in the understanding of stable economic activity (*an additive linear probabilistic image of a measured utility*).

Von Neumann – Morgenstern's proper "linear transformation" of utility was based on fantastic intuition. They state:

> ... the conceptual and practical difficulties of the notion of utility and particularly of *the attempts to describe it as a number* are well known: we shall nevertheless *be forced* [? – *M.A.*] to discuss them; we wish to concentrate on one problem – which is not that of the measurement of utilities, as to the aim of all participants in the economic system consumers as well as entrepreneurs *is money* [2] [2].

Due to the fundamental importance of the short discussion above, it seems expedient to clarify the notion "Integral Utility Criterion." From the present author's standpoint, only one formulation can be admitted as correct: when deviations within the given ratings reflect an economic equilibrium or a tolerant trade-off *compromise* between the risk of both players in the exchange – supplier and user. Fig. 7 illustrates this general approach, where the assumed mathe-

---

[2] They are trying to avoid a tautology with regard to the measurement of utilities, and thus, to avoid the crucial "quadratic" step – "the aim of all participants" – MONEY. It is interesting that the "quadratic form" has been, up until now, almost illegal in economic theory [27].

matical expectation functions of risk (M) of both market-place sides, and the compromise parabola (with the optimal level domain), are shown. Taking the general statistical meaning of the Voltage Paradox, this commercial exchange model also seems to be general. N. Kalder's famous web-like model (Fig. 8) seems primitive to us (without summing the quadratic function for the optimal domain price of the "supply-demand" process)[3].

Figure 7

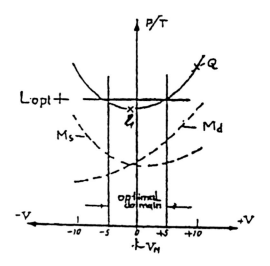

Fig. 7 **Generalized model of utility (risk) equilibrium in "two-person game"**

Ms - **rational function of supply-side risk;**
Md - **rational function of demand-side risk;**
Q - **second order curve in optimal risk domain (rational expectation range);**
L_{opt} - **stable level of exchange equilibrium, related to standard linear disutility rates (e.g., ± 5%);**
ℓ_1 - **instantaneous optimum point;**
P/T - **price/tariff axis;**
±V - **product utility criterion axis**

---

[3] Joint analysis of Figs. 7 and 8 seems to be instructive.

3.2 Disutility Additive Functional

Let us express the disutility $D_v(t)$ of the AC service voltage "exchange" stochastic process in terms of the initial second-order statistical moment for random value:

$$D_v(t) = \{M[V(t)]\}^2 + I, \qquad (23)$$

where:

$M[V(t)]$ - mathematical expectation ("regular signal");
I - nonlinear functional or the general error of the regular signal in a given dynamic system (by the impact of uncorrelated random "noises").

Then, accepting the Voltage Paradox statistical-economic substance of AC tolerant voltage ratings at delivery (e.g., ±5% deviations on V_N), the agreement of the nonviolation of its limits can be written in the following form:

Figure 8

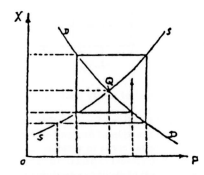

Fig. 8 **Cobweb model for supply-demand equilibrium** [7]
   S - supply quantity;
   D - demand quantity;
   X - product axis;
   P - price axis;
   Q - cobweb optimum point.

$${V_N - M[v(t)]}^2 {}_{max} + I \leq \pm V_r^2 , (\%)^2 \tag{24}$$

where

V_r – standard ratings, %;

V_N – nominal AC service voltage at delivery[4].

Hence, the voltage mode can be recognized as satisfied, if disutility as a result of voltage deviations (including random noises) is no more than at the simultaneous observance of the two following requirements:

$$0,95 \ V_N \leq M[v(t)] \leq 1,05 \ V_N \tag{25}$$

$$U = 0 \text{ (at the limit)} \tag{26}$$

The voltage utility mode, which satisfies (25) and (26), naturally satisfies (24) as well. Thus, the task is to make a quantitative estimation of the disutility functional I, that is, a series of elementary uncorrelated random functions, with:

$$M(V_v) = 0; \tag{27}$$

$$D(V_v) = M[|V_v|^2] = D_v \tag{28}$$

With regard to requirements by convergence of the variant series, the known property of the Lebesque additive measure is used.

Then, taking (28) into account, we can express:

$$I = \sum_{v=4}^{n} D_v = D_1 + D_2 + D_3 + ... + D_n . \tag{29}$$

---

[4] This formulation corresponds to Erenfest's discrete approach to the heat exchange process as analyzed by M. Kac [4].

And as applied to our problem:

$$I = D_{pn} + D_{dz} + D_{lf} + ... + \sum_{v=4}^{n} D_v,$$ (30)

where the main factors of the AC service voltage utility's random noise are:

D_{pn} variance caused by the probabilistic non-symmetry of phase voltages because of the stochastic on-off process ($\mathbf{R \equiv H}$) or ($\mathbf{GR \equiv GH}$) within a 24-hour time-dependent $\mathbf{V \equiv RB}$ model;

D_{dz} variance caused by the dead zone of the tap changing voltage control system;

D_{lf} variance caused by the stochastic process scatters of load;

$\sum_{v=4}^{n}$ total variance of the other, less important random noises [5].

With the quantitative results, which are shown in **Appendix 3.1**:

$$\mathbf{I = 2,6+0,8+0,56 = 3,96, (\%)^2},$$ (31)

or taking into account the $\sum_{v=4}^{n} \mathbf{D_v}$ reminder, the $\mathbf{V \equiv RB}$ model disutility function:

$$\mathbf{I \leq 4, (\%)^2}$$ (32)

This means that the standard deviation of the disutility $\mathbf{D_v(t)}$ stochastic function of the $\mathbf{V \equiv RB}$ model, or the significant

---

[5] Our approach to the V≡RB model disutility function (App. 3.1) can be called an economic "Kalman filter" analysis for steady-state low-frequency activity with discrete Gaussian noise ("predicted error").

random noises statistical impact, in general, is no more than (rms):

$$\bar{\sigma}_1 \leq 2\% \qquad (33)$$

Thus, the negligibly small error of the economic "Kalman filter" can be stated.

The principal claim for this study is as follows: Only one statistical characteristic – **mathematical expectation** – *for any steady-state economic activity provides a sufficiently reliable data minimum to resolve most practical problems at the normal modes of recurrent line technology in production and services.* The loss of utility (quality) for any stable recurrent economic process due to *regular random noises* is negligible. Their rigorous determination (including variance, rms, etc.) in common metric practice is justified in specific cases (e.g., for research goals). Physically, it can be explained by the nature of *stable economic information in recurrent continuous modes: stochastic sequences with a low-frequency spectrum of data components.* For this reason, *rational mathematical expectation* (mean) is the only adequate linear assessment with regard to the measurement of utility (by means of behavior analysis of measured process variables in common metric practice).

3.3 Standard Utility and Stability (customer feedback base)

In electrical technology and power production, there are a number of advanced normative documents concerning AC service voltage quality for a consumer. These are the IEC, CIGRE, and UNIPEDE recommendations concerning AC service voltage. *The integral probability of AC voltage utility, assuming a 24-hour day, is equal to the standard* **p = 0.95** [25][6]. This norm means that *the stochastic limit of a steady-state ratings violation is 72 min per calendar day.*

Regarding this point, the following key question arises: What level of power technology is needed to maintain continuously this statistical norm (supplier's risk)? And viceversa: What real *product utility* at the exchange process would be ensured by the supplier with **p = 0.95** probability level (user's risk)? Or, in general: *In this integral norm is it advisable to maintain continuous commercial equilibrium for both players: supplier and consumer?* This is the main economic issue surrounding our Voltage Paradox meaning. The answer has major importance for the general economic validity of the Voltage Paradox, and for the measurement of the crucial answer to the utility problem: *"...how should one treat situations that involve probabilities which are inevitably associated with expected utilities?"* [2]. We would suggest the same Voltage Paradox approach for the "axiomatic treatment of utility" problem. An additional model is a typical urban electrical feeder with typical urban marginal load peaks and voltage drop pattern (Fig. 9).

Points **A** and **B** in Fig. 9 are critical for estimating the commercial equilibrium in the sale of retail AC electricity, i.e., for the **p = 0.95** normative probability of voltage utility verification (that is, probabilistic treatment of the **V≡RB**

---

[6] One should hope that in the next revision of ANSI C.84.1-1995 (section 2.4), this fundamental commercial criterion will be used as in the pioneering Russian standard (GOST 13109-67, 1967) and some European valid standards (GENELEC, etc.).

general model, as well). Such an analysis seems to be correct. The residential *electrical meter* sockets are classical exchange points for modern economic process study (*"to know as much as possible about the simplest form of exchange"*) for three reasons:

(1) An essential vital commodity of continuous demand;
(2) the measurement of product utility in basic criterial and digital form;
(3) full "economic continuum," i.e., the presence of each 24-hour social biorhythm cycle (every calendar day).

The designed AC service voltage diagrams built for both external points **A** and **B** within tolerant steady-state limits are shown in Fig. 10. The background for this analysis is the non-stationarity of the **V≡RB** model (Chapter 2) and the functional assessment of its "noise" (**Appendix 3.1**). Thus, $\sigma_I[v(t)]$, as relative stationarity intervals (of the **V≡RB** model will be (see Fig. 10):

Figure 9

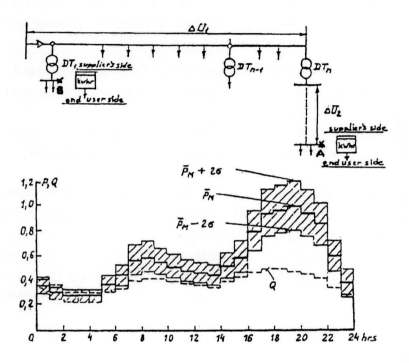

Fig. 9 Model of AC electricity exchange in two critical points.

A - commercial electrical meter with the lowest voltage (under load maximum)

B - commercial electrical meter with the highest voltage (under load minimum);

Δu - voltage loss in network elements: h.v. feeder, domestic transformer, ℓ.v. feeder (ΔU_1, ΔU_{DT}, ΔU_{DT}, ΔU_2)

P,Q - active and reactive load pattern per day;

$P_m \pm 2\sigma$ - active load statistical levels

σ̄ (Discrete general rms, %)

Points Intervals	end user lead - in Point A σ̄ (rms)	end user lead - in Point B σ̄ (rms)
Night (T_1)	1.2	0.8
Day (T_2)	1.5	1.0
Evening (T_3)	2.0	1.3

The final five tables of standard utility stability verification for the **V≡RB** general model (24-hour social biorhythm cycle) in the extremal points of AC electricity retailing are shown in **Appendix 3.2**. Let us consider the results:

Table 3.2-1 (± 5% V_N limits), client A - the total 24-hour **V≡RB** cycle violations are 53.5 min (< 72 min).

Table 3.2-2 (± 5% V_N limits), client B - the total 24-hour **V≡RB** cycle violations are 286.5 min (>> 72 min), which is unacceptable.

Table 3.2-3 (± 4-5 % V_N limits), client B – 82 min (> 72 min), but it is acceptable.

Table 3.2-4 (+ 4-5,5 % V_N limits), client A - 66 min (< 72 min).

Table 3.2-5 (+ 4-6 % V_N limits), client A - 98 min (> 72 min)[7]. Graphic determination of the design range for the **V≡RB** model utility is shown in Fig. 11, which is based on the tables of **Appendix 3.2**. One can see that **p_I=0.95** is a normative probabilistic level of commercial equilibrium for the two players of risk: supplier and consumer. Fig. 11 illustrates

---

[7] Probabilistic stability verification does not mean the invalidity of tolerant, *standard* range (± 5%, ± 6%, etc.) as basic statistical-economic ratings.

Figure 10

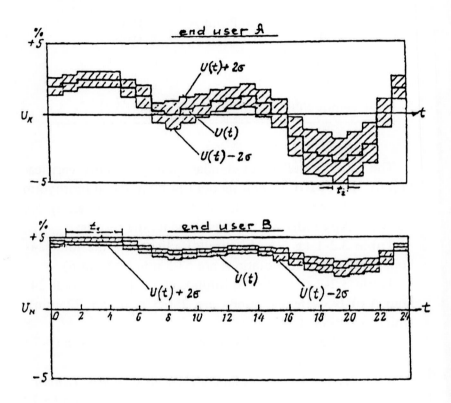

Fig. 10   AC voltage average function per calendar day (within tolerant range of disutility ±5%) in two critical points of .exchange (A,B). Form for tables (App. 3.2).

that the measurement of the rational expectation of utility is thoroughly justified and accessible to anyone who cares to check its correctness for every measured signal with a stable recurrent essence.

Fig. 11 illustrates the normative standard range of disutility which should be no more than 0.5 – 0.6 % due to regular random "noises". For other commodities, services, or manufacturing processes with other integral (economic) criteria (*temperature, pressure, speed, etc.*), our treatment is valid too. General standard probability of utility **p=0.95**, means commercial stability (*if our 3-D linear-discrete stochastic V≡RB model and its stability assessment are true*).

Figure 11

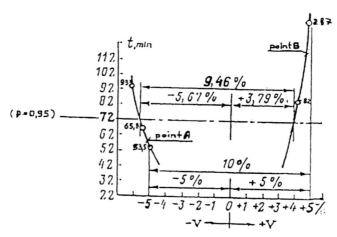

Fig. 11   The V=RB model stability verification under standard p=0.95 for process utility (with current "noise" expectation shortage of 5% admissible disutility: 10-9.46 = 0.54%). Result of App. 3.2 analysis.

It is known (from the time of Laplas and Bernoulli), that a calculation of mathematical expectation for any random process utility, in the true Bayesian sense, is impossible; the only real option is to calculate its approximate estimation (asymptotic unbiased assessment), as a realization of the finite sampling. However, our approach – standard probability of utility $p=0,95$ for any stable recurrent/ economic signal – means, that the confident assessment of mathematical/rational expectation of utility is its linear average number within the standard tolerant (integral) criterion ($\pm V_N$, %).

Thus, the correctness of our approach (according to the Voltage Paradox statistical meaning) has been verified by means of disutility additive functional quantitative assessment and its probabilistic stability near standard $p = 0.95$ (Appendices 3.1 and 3.2). This fundamental norm should be used in quality standards *as a base for customer feedback instruments and information* (N. Wiener's problem solution). International standard ISO-9000 (ISO-9004) includes this requirement (§7.3), that is a crucial step to quality problem's instrumental solution (instead of academic guides for industrial managers).

Disutility Functional Assessment

General

It is known that any stable random process can be analysed by combining three additive uncorrelated "descriptive functions":

1. harmonic component;
2. transition function (hysteresis, dead zone, and their combination);
3. fluctuations at bend points.

In our case, AC voltage descriptive functions at the delivery are:

1. the probabilistic nonsymmetry. It reflects the varying intensity of the V≡RB social biorhythm; its desired variance is D_{PN};
2. the dead zone of the voltage controller. It reflects a probabilistic impact of the voltage transition from the Gaussian distribution phase to another; its desired variance is D_{dz};
3. random spread of voltage at the peak-load time of day; its desired variance is D_{LF}.

The desired non-linear functional $I = D_{pn} + D_{da} + D+_{lf}$ means a general quadratic error ("noise") of the analysed 3D stochastic V≡RB model.

Determination of D_{pn}

Instantaneous AC voltage deviation at the sockets of a one-phase receiver is

$$V_{pn} = |U_0|\sin\alpha \qquad\qquad (A3.1\text{-}1)$$

The modulus $|U_0|$ and an angle α, are statistically independent values. All α are equiprobable ($0 < \alpha < 2\pi$). Assuming that $|U_0| = |\bar{U}_0|$, the conditional density of distribution can be written as $\varphi_0(V_{pn})$, based on (A3.1-1).

Then

$$\varphi(V_{pn}) = A \frac{d\alpha}{dV_{pn}}$$ (A3.1-2)

in the range $-\bar{U}_0 \leq U_{pn} \leq \bar{U}_0$, where A – the ratio factor. Beyond this range $\varphi_0(V_{pn}) = 0$.

The function which is inverse to (A3.1-1) within the $(0 - 2\pi)$ range has two values:

$$\alpha_1 = \text{arc sin } [V_{pn} / |U_0|)$$ (A3.1-3)

$$a_2 = \pi - \alpha_1$$ (A3.1-4)

Then, $d\alpha_1/Vd_{pn} = d\alpha_2/dV_{pn} = \dfrac{1}{dV_{pn}d\alpha} = \dfrac{1}{|U_0| \cos \alpha}$ (A3.1-5)

Taking into account (A3.1-2) and (A3.1-5) we obtain:

$$\varphi_0(V_{pn}) = \frac{A}{|U_0| \cos \alpha} = \frac{A}{\sqrt{|U_0|}^2 - V_{pn}^2}$$ (A3.1-6)

$$A = \frac{1}{\pi}$$ (A3.1-7)

Hence

$$\varphi_0(V_{pn}) = \frac{1}{\pi\sqrt{|U_0|^2 - V_{pn}^2}}$$ (A3.1-8)

The laws of V_{pn} distribution within the range $-\bar{U}_0 \leq V_{pn} \leq \bar{U}_0$, which correspond to expression (A3.1-8) are shown in Fig. 12. In the limits indicated,

if $V_{pn} \leq -\bar{U}_0$, $F_0(V_{pn}) = 0$;

if $V_{pn} \geq +\bar{U}_0$, $F_0(V_{pn}) = 1$;

$$\text{if} - \bar{U}_0 \leq V_{pn} + \bar{U}F_0(V_{pn}) = \frac{1}{2} + \frac{1}{\pi}\left(\arcsin\left(\frac{V_{pn}}{|U_0|}\right)\right) \qquad \text{(A3.1-9)}$$

The conditional distribution obtained $\varphi_0(V_{pn})$ (at $\bar{U}_0 |= \bar{U}_0|$) is practically identical to the well-known probabilities density distribution of the instantaneous values of sinusoidal voltage with a random phase. The lowest density conforms to the lowest ordinate $\frac{1}{\pi}$ $|V_{pn}|$, and the highest density at $V_{pn} \to \pm \bar{U}_0$ tends to ∞.

The average voltage deviation at one-phase receiver's sockets provided $|U_0 = | \bar{U}_0|$ is equal to:

$$|V_{pn}| = M\|V_{pn}\| = 2\int_0^{\bar{u}_0} \varphi(V_{pn})V_{pn}dV_{pn} = \frac{2}{\pi}|\bar{U}_0|. \qquad \text{(A3.1-10)}^{8}$$

Unconditional distribution (V_{pn}) with $|U_0| = |\bar{U}_0|$ and a big number of receivers can be approximated by the Gaussian law [19]. Then

$$|V_{pn}| = \int_{-\pi}^{\infty} \varphi(V_{pn})V_{pn}dV_{pn} = \frac{2}{\sqrt{2\pi\sigma}}e^{-\frac{V_{pn}}{2\sigma^2}}V_{pn}dV_{pn} = \sqrt{\frac{2}{\pi}}\sigma_{pn} \qquad \text{(A3.1-11)}$$

Comparing (A3.1-10) and (A3.1-11), we reach the final relationship

$$\sigma_{pn} = \sqrt{\frac{2}{\pi}}|\bar{U}_0| = 0.8|\bar{U}_0| \qquad \text{(A3.1-12)}$$

---

[8] Another way for determining the average value modulus $|V_{pn}|$, using the properties of mathematical expectation operation for independent quantities ($|U_0|$ and α), is:

$$|\bar{V}_{pn}| = M\|V_{pn}\|_{|U_0|=|\bar{U}_0|} = |\bar{U}_0| \cdot |\sin\alpha| = M\|U_0| \cdot |\sin\alpha|)$$

To calculate the quantity $|\sin\alpha|$ we do not need to know its distribution law. Using the condition of α equiprobability, we have:

$$\overline{|\sin\alpha|} = \frac{1}{2\pi}\int_{-\pi}^{\pi}\sin\alpha d\alpha = \frac{2}{\pi};$$

From this

$$|\bar{V}_{pn}| = \frac{2}{\pi}|\bar{U}_0|.$$

Figure 12

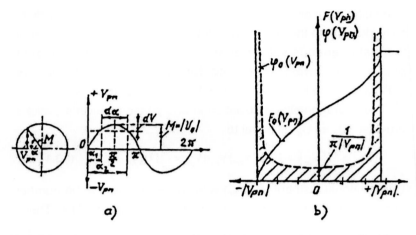

Fig. 12 D_{pn}: V_{pn} zero sequence random asymmetry shaping under random phase loads.

a) rotating-sinusoidal sweep; M-modulus of vector $|U_0|$;

b) probabilistic distribution (differential and integral laws).

The desired variance

$$D_{pn} = [0,8|\overline{U_0}|]^2 \qquad\qquad (A3.1\text{-}13)$$

Field measurements of the currents and voltage asymmetry in urban low-voltage networks showed that in general, the value $|U_0|$ at the end of a typical feeder is 2% [19].[9] According to (A3.1-13):

$$D_{pn} = 2.56(\%)^2 \qquad\qquad (A3.1\text{-}14)$$

We assume

$$D_{pn} = 2.6(\%)^2 \qquad\qquad (A3.1\text{-}15)$$

---

[9] In the case of a powerful one-phase receiver, the value $|\overline{U_0}|$ will rise.

The obtained D_{pn} is a term in a total assessment of the expression (31).

Determination of D_{dz}

We investigate the stable process of the AC voltage control system at the relative stationary interval of 3D stochastic $V \equiv$ RB model. This fully conforms to the engineering analysis of the $V \equiv$ RB. The shape of the curve U_C in comparison with U_{NC} changes basically in transitional periods under the control process (Fig. 13).

The continuous close-loop feedback is determined by on-load tap changer negative statism based on Ohm law. The jaw of this controller is described by the Ohm law linearity. Due to the dead zone and time delay, however, it has a non-linear characteristic. It makes possible consideration of the control system as the element of an economic "Kalman filter" (due to the low-frequent stable random signal of $V \equiv$ RB model with per-day transitive operation, as Fig. 4 and 13 illustrate). Therefore, the difficulty is to estimate a current random "noise" with $p(V_{in})$ during phase transition through the non-linear controller (i.e., by violating the superposition principle).

The basic problem is to determine the voltage density $p(V_{out})$ after the controller, i.e., its variance, D_{dz}.

Additional conditions should be introduced before $p(V_{out})$ construction:

1. $p(V_{in})$ is approximated by Gaussian law (within the boundaries of in the given stationary interval (Fig. 5);
2. the range is determined with the accuracy of up to c/2, where c - a regulated voltage elementary step (%);
3. $c < \varepsilon < 2c$ (ε – dead zone, %);
4. the controller is supposed to act instantaneously (without time delay);

Figure 13

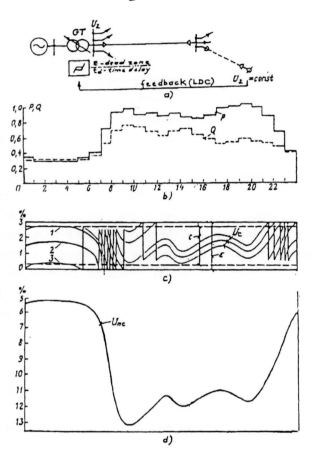

Fig. 13 D_{dz}: controlled (U) and uncontrolled (U_{nc}) high
voltage realizations per 24-hour day
a)   economic "Kalman filter" element (tap-changer
controller);
b)   load pattern of GT (grid transformer);
c)   U realizations within dead zone (ε=3%); control
step, c = 2,5%;
d) U_{nc} under load without controller

5. If two different V_{out} values conform to some V_{in} value within the limits of ε, then V_{out} values are considered as equiprobable. The segments of curve $p(V_{in})$, coinciding with the boundary ε in zone ε-c (Fig. 14), correspond to these values.

These conditions are confirmed by specific concrete voltage realization behavior (Fig. 13) in the stable and unstable controller status zone (close to the zone ε boundary before its action toward upper or lower voltage). Curves **$p(V_{in})$** and **$p(V_{out})$**, built in the boundaries of the in-out segment of relative stationarity with specific parameters, are shown in Figs. 14 and 15. Curve **$p(V_{in})$** represents the distribution of the input voltage deviations without taking into account its static character and with its position on the optimal step (c). Curve **$p(V_{out})$** represents the desired density. The case of coincidence of **$M[V_{in}(t)]$** within step (c) on this time segment is also shown.

Fig. 15 shows construction for a more general case when values of $M[V_{in}(t)]$ and "c" do not coincide (by no more than c/2). As can be seen, the essence of the analysis is a graphic integration of segments on curve (V_{in}) with different probabilities included in the desired distribution $p(V_{out})$. The integration shows that accepted assumption out curve $p(V_{out})$ represents a broken step-form function:

Step I

$$0 < |V_{out}| < c - \varepsilon/2 \qquad\qquad \text{(A3.1-16)}$$

For this range the definite value of V_{out} corresponds to each value of V_{in}. Here

$$p_I(V_{out}) \approx 1/c \qquad\qquad \text{(A3.1-17)}$$

Step II

$$c - \varepsilon/2 < |V_{out}| < \varepsilon/2.$$

For this range two equiprobable values of **V_{out}** correspond to each out

Figure 14

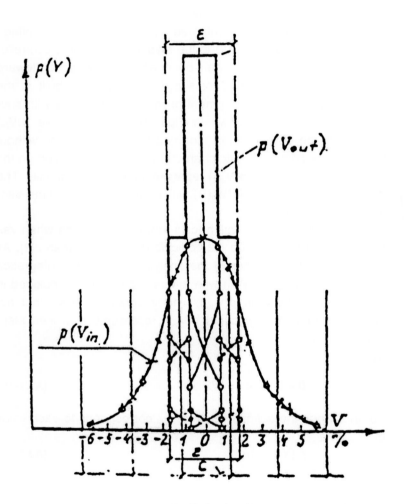

Fig. 14 D_{dz}: voltage distribution densities $p(V_{in})$ and $p(V_{out})$ under control. Coincidence of mathematical expectations.
Specific lines – for graphic integration $p(V_{in})$ zones of equal probabilities for $p(V_{out})$.

Figure 15

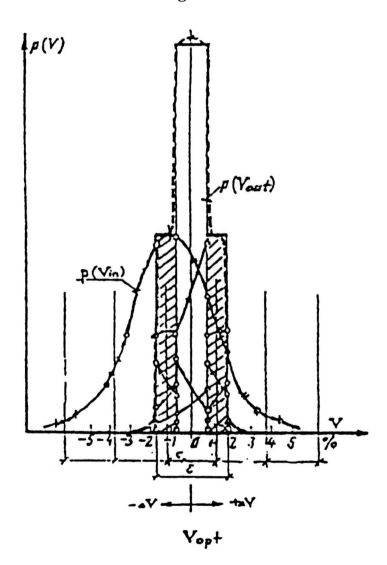

Fig. 15   D$_{dz}$: voltage distribution densities p(V$_{in}$) and p(V$_{out}$)
under control. General position.

value of V_{in}. Here

$$p_{II}(V_{out}) \approx 1/2c \qquad\qquad\qquad \text{(A3.1-18)}$$

Step III

$$s/2 < |V_{out}|$$

Here

$$p_{III}(V_{out}) = 0 \qquad\qquad\qquad \text{(A3.1-19)}$$

Within the boundaries of each step

$$p(V_{out}) = \text{const.} \qquad\qquad\qquad \text{(A3.1-20)}$$

The shape of $p(V_{out})$ depends slightly on curve $p(V_{in})$ variance and on the particular value of $M[V_{in}(t)]$ within the boundaries of $\pm$ $c/2$; as additional constructions show, such dependence becomes apparent only at the lowest values of $p(V_{in})$ distribution variation, when the problem loses, in fact, its probabilistic character.

Finally, variance D_{dz} of obtained function $p(V_{out})$ is defined from the equation:

$$D_{dz} = 2\int_{0}^{c-\frac{\varepsilon}{2}} V^2 p_I(V)dV + 2\int_{c-\frac{\varepsilon}{2}}^{\frac{\varepsilon}{2}} V^2 p_{II}(V)dv =$$

$$= \frac{2}{c}\int_{0}^{c-\frac{\varepsilon}{2}} V^2 dV + \frac{1}{c}\int_{c-\frac{\varepsilon}{2}}^{\frac{\varepsilon}{2}} V^2 dv. \qquad \text{(A3.1-21)}$$

Resolving (A3.1-21) we come to the final formula:

$$D_{dz} = \frac{\varepsilon^3 + (2c - \varepsilon)^3}{24c} \cdot (\%)^2 \qquad\qquad \text{(A3.1-22)}$$

This expression is an inexplicit function of two variables, for which only numerical solutions are possible. However, it can be resolved in a parametrical form, using the auxiliary relationship between ε and **c**. Expression (A3.1-22) at the optimal relationship between ε and **c** (ε/c=1.2÷1.5) is described with sufficient accuracy by the quadratic parabola equation:

$$\mathbf{D}_{dz} = (0,063 \div 0,065)\varepsilon^2. \tag{A3.1-23}$$

Fig. 16 presents a group of curves $D_{dz} = f(\varepsilon,c)$, which express statistical dependence of controlled signal quality on the dead zone. As can be seen, with the accepted values of c and ε the impact of the latter on the available range of voltage standard at delivery is quite small and can be neglected. For example, with **c=2.5%** and ε = **3.5%** we obtain:

$$\mathbf{D}_{dz} = 0.8(\%)^2 - \text{see (31) too} \tag{A3.1-24}$$

With the control voltage steps equal to 1,0 ÷ 1,5% , variation of D_{dz} will be twice as low.

Note that expression (A3.1-24) yields a slightly lower result than expression $\mathbf{D}_{dz}=\varepsilon^2/12$, which was obtained with the assumption that distribution $\mathbf{p(V_{out})}$ in the dead zone ε is equiprobable. The shape of the assumed distribution curves for the different relationships between c and ε is shown in Fig. 17.

In conclusion, it is necessary to add that some of the above-mentioned preconditions are not absolutely stringent: the controller operates with a noticeable time delay; the two possible values of $\mathbf{V_{out}}$, which correspond to the same value of $\mathbf{V_{In}}$, will not always be equiprobable. Taking these factors into account, curve $\mathbf{p(V_{out})}$ is built continuous with less sharp transitions between steps out of different density (see Fig. 15). Validity of expression (A3.1-22), however, cannot be affected essentially. Additional analysis shows/proves that various values of ε and c in the boundaries of **c<ε<2c** will not change the final result (A3.1-22). The analytical conclusion obtained was tested in a network operation. The coincidence of the theoretical and experimental values of $\mathbf{D}_{dz}$ is satisfactory [19].

Figure 16

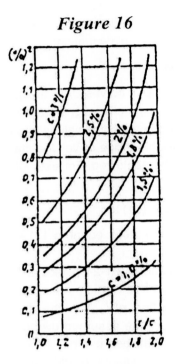

Fig. 16 D_{dz}: **Statistical impact** $D_{dz} = f(\varepsilon/c)$.

Determination of D_{lf}

The peak load (p) is a random process with basic numerical characteristics $\bar{M}$ and $\bar{\sigma}_p$, and the latter is approximately equal to $0.1\bar{M}$. Fluctuations in the peak load lead to additional voltage drops, which are characterized, for the most remote receiver, by D_{lf} value of additional voltage drop, which is equal to:

$$D_{lf} = \frac{\sigma_p}{P}(\Delta U_{DT} + \Delta U_2) = \frac{0,1\bar{M}}{P}(\Delta U_{DT} + \Delta U_2) =$$

$$= 0,083(\Delta U_{DT} + \Delta U_2). \qquad (A3.1\text{-}25)$$

Assuming the design voltage drop in the domestic transformer ($\Delta U_{DT}=2.5\%$) and in low-voltage line ($\Delta U_2=6.5\%$), the following is obtained:

$$\bar{\sigma} = 0.75\%$$ (A3.1-26)

or, going over to variance

$$D_{lf} = 0.56(\%)^2 \text{ (see (31) too.}$$ (A3.1-27)

Figure 17

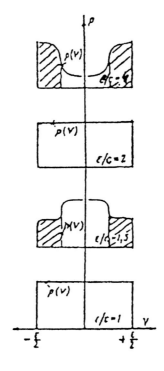

Fig. 17 D_{ez}: Distribution densities under different ε/c ratio (1; 1,5; 2; 4).

Probabilistic Stability Tables (1÷5)

Table A3.2-1

24-hour cycle	rms $\bar{\sigma}$, %	t (multiply)	$\Phi(v)$ probability of utility	$\frac{\Phi'(V)=1-\Phi(V)}{2}$ probabiity of disutility	T, min disutility process
			Point A (V=± 5%)		
T_1					
0-1	1.2	2.5	0.9876	0.0062	0.36
1-2	1.2	2.4	0.9836	0.0082	0.48
2-3	1.2	2.2	0.9722	0.0139	0.84
3-4	1.2	2.2	0.9722	0.0139	0.84
4-5	1.2	2.2	0.9722	0.0139	0.84
5-6	1.2	2.7	0.9930	0.0035	0.21
6-7	1.2	3.0	0.9973	0.0013	0.07
7-8	2.0	2.4	0.9836	0.0082	0.5
8-9	2.0	2.5	0.9876	0.0062	0.36
9-10	2.0	2.3	0.9785	0.0107	0.6
T_2					
10-11	1.5	2.9	0.9962	0.0016	0.1
11-12	1.5	2.7	0.9930	0.0035	0.21
12-13	1.5	2.7	0.9930	0.0035	0.32
13-14	1.5	2.5	0.9876	0.0062	0.36
14-15	1.5	2.8	0.9948	0.0029	0.18
15-16	1.5	3.3	0.9990	0.0005	0.03
T_3					
16-17	2.0	1.6	0.9809	0.0505	3.0
17-18	2.0	1.1	0.7286	0.1357	8.1
18-19	2.0	1.03	0.6826	0.1577	9.5
19-20	2.0	0.83	0.5934	0.2033	12.0
20-21	2.0	1.0	0.6826	0.1587	9.5
21-22	2.0	1.4	0.8385	0.0808	4.8
22-23	2.0	2.5	0.9876	0.0062	0.36
23-24	1.2	2.7	0.9930	0.0035	0.21
Total for 24-hour cycle					53.49

Table A3.2-2

24-hour cycle	rms $\bar{\sigma}$, %	t (multiply)	$\Phi(v)$ probability of utility	$\frac{\Phi'(V)=1-\Phi(V)}{2}$ probability of disutility	T, min disutility process
\multicolumn{6}{c}{Point B (V=± 5%)}					
T_1					
0-1	0.8	0.25	0.1974	0.4013	24.0
1-2	0.8	0.125	0.1000	0.4500	27.0
2-3	0.8	0.125	0.1000	0.4500	27.0
3-4	0.8	0.125	0.1000	0.4500	27.0
4-5	0.8	0.125	0.1000	0.4500	27.0
5-6	0.8	0.5	0.3829	0.3085	18.5
6-7	0.8	0.7	0.5161	0.2419	14.5
7-8	1.3	1.0	0.6827	0.1586	9.5
8-9	1.3	1.1	0.7287	0.1356	8.1
9-10	1.3	1.0	0.6827	0.1586	9.5
T_2					
10-11	1.0	1.0	0.6827	0.1586	9.5
11-12	1.0	1.0	0.6825	0.1356	8.1
12-13	1.0	0.9	0.6319	0.1840	11.1
13-14	1.0	0.9	0.6319	0.1840	11.1
14-15	1.0	1.0	0.6827	0.1586	9.5
15-16	1.0	1.1	0.7287	0.1356	8.1
T_3					
16-17	1.3	1.4	0.8385	0.0808	4.8
17-18	1.3	1.8	0.9281	0.0359	2.2
18-19	1.3	1.9	0.9426	0.0287	1.7
19-20	1.3	2.1	0.9643	0.0178	1.08
20-21	1.3	2.0	0.9543	0.0227	1.35
21-22	1.3	1.9	0.9426	0.0287	1.71
22-23	1.3	1.4	0.8385	0.0808	4.8
23-24	0.8	0.5	0.3829	0.3085	18.5
\multicolumn{5}{c}{Total for 24-hour cycle}					286.53

Table A3.2-3

24-hour cycle	rms $\bar{\sigma}$, %	t (multiply)	Φ(v) probability of utility	$\frac{\Phi'(V)=1-\Phi(V)}{2}$ probability of disutility	T, min disutility process
Point B (V=± 4-5%)					
T_1					
0-1	0.8	1.5	0.8664	0.0668	4.0
1-2	0.8	1.38	0.8324	0.0810	4.7
2-3	0.8	1.38	0.8324	0.0810	4.7
3-4	0.8	1.38	0.8324	0.0810	4.7
4-5	0.8	1.38	0.8324	0.0810	4.7
5-6	0.8	1.75	0.9199	0.0405	2.4
6-7	0.8	1.78	0.9249	0.0376	2.3
7-8	1.3	1.0	0.6827	0.1586	9.5
8-9	1.3	1.1	0.7287	0.1356	8.1
9-10	1.3	1.0	0.6827	0.1586	9.5
T_2					
10-11	1.0	2.1	0.9643	0.0178	1.08
11-12	1.0	2.1	0.9643	0.0178	1.08
12-13	1.0	2.0	0.9545	0.0227	1.35
13-14	1.0	2.0	0.9545	0.0227	1.35
14-15	1.0	2.1	0.9643	0.0178	1.08
15-16	1.0	2.1	0.9643	0.0178	1.08
T_3					
16-17	1.3	1.4	0.8385	0.0808	4.8
17-18	1.3	1.8	0.9281	0.0359	2.2
18-19	1.3	1.9	0.9426	0.0287	1.7
19-20	1.3	2.1	0.9643	0.0178	1.08
20-21	1.3	2.0	0.9543	0.0227	1.35
21-22	1.3	1.9	0.9426	0.0287	1.71
22-23	1.3	1.4	0.8385	0.0808	4.8
23-24	0.8	2.4	0.8904	0.0505	3.0
Total for 24-hour cycle					82.25

Table A3.2-4

24-hour cycle	rms $\bar{\sigma}$, %	t (multiply)	$\Phi(v)$ probability of utility	$\frac{\Phi'(V) = 1 - \Phi(V)}{2}$ probability of disutility	T, min disutility process
Point A (V=+ 4-5,5%)					
T_1					
0-1	1.2	2.9	0,.9962	0.0002	0.1
1-2	1.2	2.8	0.9948	0.0029	0.18
2-3	1.2	2.6	0.9707	0.0046	0.27
3-4	1.2	2.6	0.9907	0.0046	0.27
4-5	1.2	2.6	0.9907	0.0046	0.27
5-6	1.2	3.1	0.9973	0.0013	0.07
6-7	1.2	3.4	0.9993	0.0003	0.02
7-8	2.0	2.7	0.9930	0.0035	0.21
8-9	2.0	2.8	0.9948	0.0029	0.18
9-10	2.0	2.6	0.9907	0.0046	2.7
T_2					
10-11	1.5	3.3	0.9990	0.0005	0.3
11-12	1.5	3.1	0.9980	0.0001	0.6
12-13	1.5	3.1	0.9980	0.0001	0.6
13-14	1.5	2.9	0.9962	0.0002	0.1
14-15	1.5	3.2	0.9986	0.0007	0.04
15-16	1.5	3.7	0.9998	0.0001	0.01
T_3					
16-17	2.0	1.4	0.8385	0.0808	4.8
17-18	2.0	0.9	0.6319	0.1840	12.0
18-19	2.0	0.8	0.5934	0.2033	12.0
19-20	2.0	0.63	0.4515	0.2742	16.0
20-21	2.0	0.8	0.5934	0.2033	12.0
21-22	2.0	1.2	0.7698	0.1201	7.2
22-23	2.0	2.3	0.9785	0.0107	0.6
23-24	1.2	3.1	0.9980	0.0001	0.06
Total for 24-hour cycle					65.8

Table A3.2-5

24-hour cycle	rms ϩ, %	t (multiply)	Φ(v) probability of utility	$\frac{\Phi'(V)=1-\Phi(V)}{2}$ probability of disutility	T, min disutility process
Point A (V=+ 4-6%)					
T₁					
0-1	1.2	3.3	0.9990	0.0005	0.903
1-2	1.2	3.2	0.9986	0.0007	0.042
2-3	1.2	3.0	0.9973	0.0013	0.07
3-4	1.2	3.0	0.9973	0.0013	0.07
4-5	1.2	3.0	0.9973	0.0013	0.07
5-6	1.2	3.5	0.9995	0.0002	0.01
6-7	1.2	3.8	0.9998	0.0001	0.006
7-8	2.0	2.9	0.9962	0.0016	0.1
8-9	2.0	3.0	0.9973	0.0013	0.07
9-10	2.0	2.8	0.9948	0.0029	0.18
T₂					
10-11	1.5	3.6	0.9996	0.0002	0.01
11-12	1.5	3.4	0.9993	0.003	0.02
12-13	1.5	3.4	0.9993	0.0003	0.02
13-14	1.5	3.2	0.9986	0.0007	0.04
14-15	1.5	3.5	0.9995	0.0002	0.01
15-16	1.5	4.0	0.9999	0.0005	0.001
T₃					
16-17	2.0	1.1	0.7286	0.1357	8.1
17-18	2.0	0.6	0.4515	0.2742	16.5
18-19	2.0	0.5	0.3829	0.3085	18.5
19-20	2.0	0.33	0.2586	0.3707	18.5
20-21	2.0	0.5	0.3829	0.3085	18.5
21-22	2.0	0.9	0.6319	0.1840	11.1
22-23	2.0	2.0	0.9545	0.0227	1.35
23-24	1.2	3.5	0.9995	0.0002	0.02
Total for 24-hour cycle					98.3

94

CHAPTER 4

The "Stability and Utility" Concept

We need a new approach.
J. Forrester, 1961

POSTULATE

Any stable data subset hyperplane for economic line-recurrent stochastic status (vector or scalar sequence) is correlated in space with one of the saddle vicinities by the orbit-rotational Earth trajectory in Newton–Lagrange–Hamilton second order metrics.

AXIOMS

(1) The basic cycle (BC) for the recurrent process of any economic value dynamics is a 24-hour calendar day (rational behavior or social biorhythm cycle): the behavioristic control loop.

(2) Each BC includes several convex subsets of stability and utility-measured data, which have an economic content. Each subset contains its local optimum. General object function does not exist.

(3) Each BC realization of the recurrent parameter in any line business (production or service) is a stable stochastic

signal with the low frequency spectrum of four discrete data series/files. Each stable subset of data requires the linear programming and/or linear regression's optimization procedures only.

(4) Each BC stable recurrent stochastic signal relates to the Markovian essential time-dependent sequence, which satisfies the Lebesque additive measure (L^2) and the Gibbs quasi-ergodic hypothesis. This includes data intervals/segments of a relative time-independent process (stationary in a wide sense), on which every discrete density is close to Gaussian approximation.

(5) The stable recurrent stochastic signal constraints within each BC are regular (Kuhn–Tacker term treatment).

(6) For each stable recurrent analog signal, the second order disutility functional presence is ensured on each data convex subset within the BC. This functional economic "noise" impact in normal operation is negligibly small in tolerant standard steady-state range for this signal's random fluctuations.

(7) For each quantitative measured parameter or stable recurrent qualitative analog signal, a real measure of its cardinal utility in production and services is a linear-discrete digital unit: Sum or Mean (arithmetic aver-

96

age/rational expectation), i.e., one number as an adequate utility discrete presentation on each data convex subset within BC (with <u>one rational saddle point/local optimum</u>).

(8) For each stable recurrent analog signal within each BC, there are two essentially separate security criteria:

    a. Dynamic stability or metabolism (existence), which does not possess the optimization object function for raising its utility (internal constants).
    For example: Earth rotation velocity, gravitation constant, market equilibrium, AC frequency, temperature of a being, assembly line speed, etc.

    b. Steady-state parametric stability or homeostasis (feedback), which possesses the optimization object function for raising its utility (external parameters).
    For example: tolerant standard steady-state range (an integral criterion) of external analog signals (AC service voltage, pressure, temperature), commodity price, a being's response, etc.

(9) Maintenance of metabolism (existence) is a vital goal of any stable recurrent status in production and services. Its normative confident probability $p = 1.0$ during each BC, or within a vital control loop activity. Commercial

sanctions for normal operation interruptions depend on contract terms.

(10) Maintenance of homeostasis (feedback) is an exchange goal of any stable recurrent status in production and services (for commercial equilibrium). Its normative confident probability p=0.95 during each BC or within behavioristic control loops activity with normative quality.

(11) Any predetermined change of p=0.95 standard probability is the subject of a special contract and is supplied and paid by the customer.

(12) Delay, distortion, or absence of reliable information about the current metabolism (existence) and homeostasis (feedback) criteria of a stable rational economic status are under supply-side responsibility.

CHAPTER 5

Concluding Remarks

5.1 The Voltage Paradox

> Economy is too complicated. It can't be formulated in a general model. It will very probably not be solved during our lifetime. There is a little hope that it will be settled by the usual methods because of the enormous complexity.
>
> *J. von Neumann, O. Morgenstern, 1944*

> A mathematical model should be based on the best information. That day will never come.
>
> *J. Forrester, 1961*

> Economics is a non experimental discipline.
>
> *L. Klein, 1962*

> Model-building is the essence of the management science approach.
>
> *H. Wagner, 1970*

> The concept of rational expectations is old in economics. Budding economists want a method for generating scholarly publications.
>
> I confidently predict that the subject of rational expectations will supply another element in this collection of things, which did not provide a breakthrough. Econometric models do not provide the only approach for all problems.
>
> *L. Klein, 1983[1]*

---

[1] J. Wanniski's "silent scream", purebred professional feedback is worth mentioning here. He argues a concept that people are "as uniform as

...the overall objective is still the same – the basis in the fundamentals of data base technology.

C. Date, 1986

For over two hundred years, economists, mathematicians and philosophers have been active in formulating theories of rational behavior.

J. Eatwell, M. Milgate, P. Newman, 1990

The need to go is apparent, but where to go is less clear.

A. Sen, 1990

It is impossible to write down any standard procedure that should always be followed.

F. Hiller, G. Lieberman, 1990

We stress that art topics are most useful in the analysis of practical problems.

H.A. Taha, 1992

I cannot imagine how we could possibly organize and make use of the mass of data without model building.

R. Lucas, 1993

A more optimistic opinion is presented by A. Harvey [28]:

---

hydrogen molecules" for an econometric model, which does not work. "Why does the economics profession have so little to show for its skills?" [30]. References [31-44], including [24], reflect this conceptual long-term deadlock (50 years) among professionals in database technology: software crisis for macroeconomy's data general model.

The issues raised by the problem of model selection are extremely complex, and it would be foolish to pretend that there is a generally acceptable solution, which can be applied in most cases.

There is an increasing awareness of the potential of optimal control in econometrics.

A. Harvey, 1990

The above quotations by some of the 20th century's most brilliant intellectuals are cited for a single reason:

To emphasize that the "voltage paradox" as an analytical tool for this inaccessible statistical-economic study is such a specifically "electrical" approach that, not by mere chance, it was utterly beyond these prominent scholars' collective intellect.

However, it must be stressed that J. von Neumann and O. Morgenstern possessed fantastic intuition; it was perfectly monumental. More to the point, both of them and I. Good predicted the Voltage Paradox as a general statistical background (Chapter 1), a new paradigm for a stable lifeline statistical-economic analysis in post-industrial developed society. This "naive outsider's idea" has apparently produced the only adequate philosophical tool for a real solution. About one hundred years ago, N. Tesla understood the *physical* might of AC electricity; the next electrical engineer (J. Chervonenkis) was fortunate enough to understand its *statistical* might[2].

---

[2] The fatal error of econometrics in the field of public utilities [20] is its single analytical base: the AC load current behavior study (load management theory), which kills a cybernetic approach to the commercial supply-demand process.

Firstly, we are fortunate to guess that the humanoid's day-to-day electrical "on-off" activity at any given place, measured by an electrical meter, is *the most universal "supermarket" for the simplest "two-person game"/commercial exchange marketplace.*

Secondly, this quite simple exchange is connected with classical second order principles of stability in physics, the calculus of variations, and the random theory, up to the stellar dynamics postulate: "The second moments define a general symmetric tensor of the second rank" [4].

From the engineering perspective, the most significant result of this paradoxical approach: is our 3D general stochastic **V≡RB** model's validity <u>for each recurrent signal in line macrobusiness process control (from temperature up to money flow)</u>. This is a remarkably true, but non-obvious effect (statistical similarity for recurrent signal dynamics in Nature), which is conceptually equal to the strange, but true, "Plato's cave" effect [16].

5.2 3D Linear-Discrete V≡RB Model

If the **V≡RB** model is an essentially time-dependent (non-stationary) process, the need for its statistical presentation is apparent; thus, the same discrete approach applies to any stable recurrent stochastic signal/parameter in production and services (voltage, pressure, temperature, speed, vibration, etc.), i.e., in a value-creating manufacturing process.

It seems that this **V≡RB** model's meaning can be strengthened by the following argument:

> If the Earth is a value, then it follows that its reaches and resources were created <u>long before</u> the appearance of the individual's rational activity and his economic theories. A technological masterpiece – the hen's egg – is a clock-stable ellipsoid of the Earth's

rotation and dynamics; it appeared before the hen.

It can prudently be suggested that the linear-discrete presentation of the **V≡RB** model (**with four saddle points**) is just as adequate an approximation to the optimal datamation process for resources accumulating recurrent technology in Nature.

The conceptual difference between **3D** physical space and **3D** economic space, as introduced in [19], should be noted. Once more, the former contains an object's arbitrary trajectory coordinates (x,y,z); whereas the latter notion, has time-utility-probabilistic recurrent coordinates (t,u,p), in which any value dynamic characteristics can be measured, i.e., in which any stable economic status of stability and utility exists.

Logically, we can formulate the general basic principle for the 3D stochastic **V≡RB** model (with four linear data series/files) presented here (Fig. 4): *the discrete principle of security (existence and quality).*

It is known that a human being lives in an essentially anisotropic physical and social environment. Our 3D stochastic **V≡RB** model is an adequate image of an anisotropic model for every product and service utility (± spaces).

The loss of stability for this model (**p=1.0**) and normative utility maintenance (**p=0.95**) are determined by two probabilistic hyperplanes:

(1) along/stochastic – for an **internal** impact response;

(2) across/parametrical – for an **external** impact response.

On this conceptual base, we can see the proper approach to the **V≡RB** anisotropic treatment of its optimal hyper planes:

(1) along/stochastic – for macroeconomic process continuous existence/ reliability linear discrete assessment;

(2) across/parametrical – for macroeconomic process continuous quality linear discrete assessment [3].

5.3 Standard Probability of Utility

> ...no useful indications and 'a fortiori' no special instructions as to how one should treat situations that involve probabilities, which are inevitably associated with expected utilities.
>
> *J. von Neumann, O. Morgenstern, 1944*

It was their last, sad words: after 15 years of study, they had returned to the starting point – confronted by Bernoulli's St. Petersburg Paradox (1738). They are both knew that their neo-Bernoullian formulation was true for any stable economic status, but with "no useful indications," *no proper pattern* to prove this fundamental neo-Bernoullian statement. (However, what intuition!)

An adequate "voltage" answer is as follows: the standard risk-taking probability of utility for any *stable economic state* or any stable random choice in rational recurrent business, i.e., *the standard   utility* (**p=0.95**) *or disutility* (**p = 0.05**) *for line processes in macroeconomy* [4].

---

[3] There were some elegant non-linear results and theories for the business schedule and its models [18].

[4] Let us leave the "psychology of risk" to Monte Carlo casino and a gamble "scientific progress".

5.4 "Stability and Utility" Concept

In spite of a satisfactory statistical background, the "Stability and Utility" concept has been formulated as an engineering statement of the current *two-person game* business practice, as the most general case.

The initial postulate is the conceptual synthesis of causality and multi-collinear fortuity squareness in the Universe; that is the gist of the Earth's clock-ellipsoid orbit stability. On the whole, this postulate reflects the hidden, but *tough linkage* between the solar system's majestic-hostile simplicity, its fully automatic inconceivable accuracy, power, stable recurrent dynamics, and an individual's rational behavior in social macrobusiness activity.

It is well-known that the General Relativity Theory could only be understood by its genius author. But even a primitive engineering vision tells us that now is the time to "risk" and cite his most significant rational thought: "A local space curvative degree depends on the matter-mass density clustering within it".

Thus, a close correlation can be seen between the two-couple 3D interface similarity in space:

(1) Physical (matter and energy).
(2) Economic (matter and information) according to our postulate.

This similarity is an additional argument to the discussion in 5.2 regarding *the discrete time principal of stochastic stability*. In other words: If energy and information are identical notions, the general law of Nature superstable dynamics (*sampled accumulation and pulse transition*) can once more be confirmed [5].

---

[5] As a curiosity, one can recall the melancholy words of M. Kac (1946), regarding the Erenfests' (1907) discrete hypothesis for heat exchange:

Axioms 1 – 12 are bare economic "psalms" which apparently have been formulated canonic procedures on the basis of our results (Chapters 2, 3) and the initial postulate above[6]. They are applied to stable economic status, as the rational contents of human activity, which is an integral valid part of general physical principles: the digital criterial stability/code of a strict clockwork stellar dynamic system on which Earth's Nature lives and works during its evolution.

Axioms 2, 3, 4, and 5 are a practical development of the main statistical facts of the **V≡RB** model within a calendar day (basic macroeconomic cycle): Linear-discrete with **four social saddle points**/local optimums and low frequency substance, with relative and partial time-independence (stationary) under regular constraints.

In the same practical manner, axioms 9, 10, 11, and 12 constitute an instrumental criterial approach to statistical quality monitoring and financial mutual responsibility of both marketplace sides for its commercial equilibrium, which provides stability and utility's inspection possibility (existence and feedback information). Founded on an analytical basis, they can be included in specific supply-demand regulation contracts (ISO-9004 support).

Axioms 1, 6, 7, and 8 have the most profound sense as the true path to digital and standard axiomatic (social) treatment of utility. They formulate **four** subject transitions concerning

---

"The main advantages of a discrete approach are *pedagogical*" [4]. But the same M. Kac demonstrates the proper approach of P. and T. Erenfest's discrete model and the nonlinear (quadratic) measure of stability for the mean recurrence time.

[6] As G. Dantzig said: "neglect negligible" [12].

fully automatic standard macroeconomic database:

(1)   We divide its control loop for two critical aspects: vital (or metabolism) and behavioristic (or homeostasis). Each valid economic analog signal carries within itself double criterial content (dichotomy): existing and optimizing. The first (dynamic stability) means the functional life (**p=1.0**) for a system (Liapunov, Niquist criteria and others); the second – its utility (**p=0.95**) or quality (static stability). The first requires deep (down to spectral) analysis and a "holy war" with "noise" – the classic control theory's subject; the second does not deal with noise at all; its subject is a particular arithmetic mean or discrete expectation within a behavioristic control loop/ calendar day, i.e., the basic economic cycle (BC). This treatment is close to the Poincare cycle [4].

W. Mitchell's time series and cycles had no scientific meaning, because of its full ignorance of social behavior (according to T. Koopman) [14] [7].

(2)   As mentioned above, we refuse to take into account a real random noise of any recurrent analog signal, for two reasons:

a. In an optimizing sense within the BC, the economic process is not a sign-reversible function; we do not need to solve the Fourier integral. For example,

$$\frac{1}{2\pi}\int_0^\infty \tau e^{-2\pi f \tau}d\tau \quad \text{as to } \mathbf{f} \text{ is negligible for}$$

---

[7] The same "Theory of Games" ignores stochastic dynamics in its remarkable economic behavior analysis [2].

The modern econometric analysis of a time series is also ignores the stochastic approach [28].

a low-frequency spectrum.

b. Real damage (disutility) because of the impact of random noise is also negligibly small (see Appendix 3.1). The mean of a measured signal utility can be presented as a valid rational expectation in analytical procedures (mean of full signal with one saddle point). Additionally, communication effect was obtained according to Schennon's theorem: the speed and power of an economic signal transmission can be close to the theoretical limit of SNR [23].

(3)   We have proven (contrary to L. Klein) that macroeconomics (due to metrology subsystem) is an experimental discipline: A utility can and must be measured and assessed instrumentally via its rational expectation presentation as a cardinal utility criterion (via a set of standards)[8]. In J. von Neumann, O. Morgenstern's words: "up to a linear transformation" (axiom 7).

(4)   We clarified (axiom 8) one of the most nebulous conceptual problems that remained after N. Wiener's death: Interpretation of homeostasis (feedback) as a single stability criterion; apparently, this was the only error made by the intellectual giant. P. Samuelson committed the same fundamental error in nondivided statics and dynamics vision [14].

In conclusion, one can only hope that the Stability and Utility concept can be presented as a general protocol base (standard software/digital code) of OSI layers (ISO) em-

---

[8] Pareto's "indifference" works, but now only at a dinner table.

bodiment in standard four linear-discrete half-period data subsets for any stable economic status in line production and service (macroeconomy) and its two **linear** optimization procedures (simplex and regression) for each one separately.

5.5 The Innocent Partialities of the Greats

Being a sceptic, the author knows that any new approach sparks an instinctive protest[9]. Here, we attempted to apprise the reader, briefly, of some key questions that have appeared in a handful of selected works, with true intimate knowledge and the same misunderstanding in some cases, even an inexplicable prejudice. In this context, our reference list seems adequate.

5.5.1 Beware of the "Human factor"

The common base up to now is the stable "eternal progressive" vision of the **human factor's** full prerogatives in economic processes. The deadlock in robot technology has been a sure sign of a powerful trend to "focus on people" as a traditional paradigm in economics, which certainly 'works' (being well-trained and stimulated, as circus animals).

N. Wiener's idea about fully automated factories has turned out to be too advanced, but it is worthwhile recalling that his creation, cybernetics, is an informational science only[10]. And indeed, might the personal computer and various software in macroeconomics be the enemy within? [30]

---

[9] It is hard to believe that the remarkable scientific results achieved by solitary individuals in the nineteenth century should be recognized in the 20th "pieceful" second half for unknown talented outsiders (medicine-biology aside).

[10] Incidentally, N. Wiener's name has been almost completely forgotten (instead of "cybernetics," we now use the term "protocol").

The limitations of the Human Factor (or "knowledge workers") in modern 3-D line business data are obvious. The era of congenial managers and software makers is over in complex industrial production and services. Lee Iacocca was the "Last of the Mohicans." *Timely and proper measured-based* standard digital protocol in macrobusiness is an imperative current problem, but not an academic guide for managers (e.g., the famous guides for quality improvement by E. Deming, P. Drucker and M. Baldrige).

From the "Theory of Games..." up to "Utility and Probability" macroeconomic theory concentrated on a humanoids' rational behavior model formalization, that is, a true scientific problem. But productivity in large, complex business and limited human potential are not the same things today[11].

5.5.2 System or Chaos?

From the first to the very last word, von Neumann and Morgenstern's great book has left a deep impression, mainly by virtue of its brilliant constellations of prophetic notes. Nevertheless, the key notions for modern economic analysis, Criterion and Feedback, were unknown to them (according to the subject index). They could not overcome the static open-loop approach to economic reality – except as a personal game (beyond this game's stochastic dynamics)[12]. The traditional obsolete analysis of "personal preferences, psychology of risk" can be seen in almost all contemporary

---

[11] It is true, **human potential** also will define some elements of big business productivity in the high-tech age (e.g., sticky-fingered shopping or astrology).

[12] The same personal, but *"low* personal game" called business such a prophet as N. Wiener. An innocent partiality, perhaps?

economic essays up until the present day [27]. On the other hand, a correct technological approach by W. Leontief (the input-output method), J. Forrester (Dynamo flows), and V. Glushkov (industrial cybernetical *control*) did not have adequate physical support.

The decisive "astro-stochastic" background for rational behavior formalization seemed strange as "heaven-scholastic." In this context, mention must be made of at least three intellectuals who considered the macro-economy movement as a purely engineering problem: Marcus Aurelius, Thorsten Veblen, and Jacob Chervonenkis (the author's scientific guru).

Marcus Aurelius stated: "Nature is a system. The parts of the whole are everything. Observe – what Nature requires. Above all around – the movement of the elements" [13].

5.5.3 Nonlinear Boom

The "trivial" linear approach by G. Dantzig (1945) became exhausted for applied mathematicians concerned with his classical simplex procedure (the linear programming method). Therefore, the nonlinear "home-made" models and refined theorems of bright child prodigies (Bellman, Pontriagin, Samuelson, and other "armchair" thinkers) began to descend upon economics and real economic problems. The mathematical brilliance of their intellect cast a spell over naive students. The nonlinear-mathematical boom spawned hundreds of new and remarkable papers and books, confer-

---

[13] The modern guru, shaman consultants, chaos theory, and tribal culture adepts [29] should read "Meditations" by Marcus Aurelius.

Thorsten Veblen is mentioned here not by chance. He was completely correct: The manufacturing process, and **not** marketing artistry, an idle design, or money tricks is the first task towards true progress for people. Technology or Monetarism? Work or Interest Rates? – These are the most acute questions for free system stability.

ences and symposia in exotic countries; tenures; and expensive business schools – yet, its economic "weight" was in fact close to the great zero [15, 26].

An outstanding attempt to overcome this nonlinear illusional effect was undertaken by the phenomenal J. Forrester, who launched a crusade against mathematics in business management. He declared, "Mathematics is weaker than Nature" [8]. Forrester became embroiled in a 10-year battle: in his almost unerring treatment of "Industrial Dynamics", there was not a **single** mathematical formula in 456 pages.

This unique book was published in seven editions; it became the cornerstone of an "anti-mathematical" management school at MIT (perhaps because of student appeals). Forrester's intuitive approach was super-talented, but it was hopelessly close to technological lifeline "DYNAMO printouts".

5.5.4 "Measurement of Utility" puzzle

This is a classic subject in economics, the result of about one hundred years of marginal ordinal and cardinal utility theories. Our "standard probability of utility" approach is based on von Neumann–Morgenstern's numerical conception of cardinal utility. Marginal and ordinal utility notions are inherent in personal preferences and indifferences, mainly by V. Pareto's central notions. This "personal" out-of-date philosophy is invalid for systemic cybernetical vision in the modern macroeconomic hierarchy[14]. Our approach follows some basic points on which the "Stability and Utility" concept stands:

(1)   Utility and any stable recurrent signal security (its metabolism and homeostasis) are identical notions.

---

[14] "Ordinal utility" was invented after J. von Neumann's death.

(2)   A common metric practice (with its calibration, scale
        of measurement, and tolerant-statistical criteria
      of integral standards) is an adequate base for the
      proper assessment of discrete numerical utility in line
      processes, i.e., macroeconomy.
(3)   The utility's two normative probabilities (axiom 9,10)
      for resources and manufacturing processes – but not
      trade skill, design art, or monetary policy – are de-
      cisive fields for making budget money.

5.5.5 Linear Transformation again

Below, as an additional argument to utility's rational linear transformation (instead of psychology), we suggest the
discussion of two physical laws:

(1)   the interactive squareness of fundamental categories
      by Nature dynamics: matter and energy;

(2)   the complex mass motion trajectory is equal to its cen-
      tral material point trajectory.

The general squareness principle for any stable recurrent
structure means its physical parameters linear criterial presentation up to the rational expectation of utility as a versatile
cardinal assessment[15].

---

[15] R. Allen agreed that only the cardinal utility approach via the metric
"scale of utilities" can be correct. He referred to the basic points of "ex-
act sciences" metrology-zero and calibration as an example [7].

W. Baumol showed his terrible misunderstanding of the discrete-
stochastic base of a stable economic process. He wrote: "The mean is a
nonsignificant factor in optimization," and more top the point: "In linear
programming there is not any economic sense" [11].

(1)   We have never seen a paper devoted specifically to the central puzzle of the Nature philosophy: *the squareness* meaning for solar system stability (and utility), with this fundamental physical law's historical analysis (from Galileo up to Einstein's postulates).

As for the Voltage Paradox, one can remark that J. Chervonenkis and R. Pelissier's approach had a close proximity to its true economic meaning. However, Pelissier did not understand the profound sense of P. Aillerett's [5] controversial idea (his colleague in Electricité de France), and stopped just short of AC service voltage disutility complexity for measurement [17].

But Chervonenkis (also an electrical engineer) suggested an elegant hypothesis for a proper metric treatment of AC service voltage tolerant standard rates as a rational expectation image (the same "Neo-Bernoullian" approach as von Neumann–Morgenstern's). Our "Linear Transformation" analysis (Chapter 3) has verified the validity of this unobvious but true hypothesis[16].

(2)   The physical law of mass centers motion is the conceptual background of common metric practice accuracy. It postulates that only external forces can be measured and, indeed, internal structural forces cannot be measured separately[17]. As to its economic treatment, one can suppose that Bayesian unmeasured internal forces are indeed personal behavioristic categories – preference, risk, indifference, etc. However, its integral external effect under an individual's will is a real individual response: an "on-off" stochastic process via the statistical effect of the "voltage paradox".

---

[16] This remarkable hypothesis was a completely independent result (J. Chervonenkis graduated from Grenoble Polytechnic College in 1935).

[17] In "geological" economic terminology: endogenous and exogenous process variables.

Thus, each rational behavior data (axiom 7) can realize statistically the linear discrete presentation of any stable economic signal/protocol within the behavioristic control loop, i.e., <u>within each calendar day</u> (temperature, pressure, cash flow, service distribution, etc.)[18].

5.5.6 Fly to the Moon

Most impressive for us was the bestseller by L. Young, *Lectures on the Calculus of Variations and Optimal Control Theory* [16]. This book, we believe, is a sad historical case of one-sided, mathematical, innocent partiality (or "highly personal style", as W. Fleming so elegantly noted in the foreword). Being a *pure mathematician*, Young discloses his course as a fascinating detective story. He was inspired to achieve a great "practical" goal: an optimal trajectory for flying to the moon. His Optimal Control Theory, however, is based on versatile applications, including the mathematical economics (as W. Fleming accurately remarked). Furthermore, this pure thinker in the *Calculus of Variations* did not understand that his favorite Hamiltonian is a dynamic second order image of the stochastic stellar trajectory's stability and utility; he twice refuses to descend to "low" stochastic analysis from his lofty mathematical heavens[19].

Indeed, N. Wiener was a "local stochastic" philosopher,

---

[18] This second additional argument, it seems to us, indeed convinces a disclosure of von Neumann–Morgenstern's "subtle way of measuring marginal utility, more than is usually assumed" [2]. This "subtle way" version is our answer: standard probability of disutility, **p=0.05**; i.e., utility's rational expectaton validity for any measured economic signal linear-discrete presentation.

[19] It is strange, but there was not one mention of Wiener's name in L. Young's truly remarkable book. We guess that the reason was the "overly brave" title of Wiener's autobiography: *I am a Mathematician*.

but, using his perfectly supersubtle mind, he constructed a conceptual linkage between the Lebesque additive measure (L^2) and Gibbs' ergodic hypothesis, i.e. between pure thinking and real life. Our axiom 4 is based on this true intellectual enlightenment of N. Wiener.

5.6 Valid Results

We hope that the above section (5.5) has clearly demonstrated the measure of the confusion when faced with tough contradictions, which created an almost untenable conceptual deadlock in economics. Some remarkable "Utility and Probability" essays seem to be an elegant gravestone of this discipline [27].

However, an active and fortuitous professional life in engineering has enabled us to work for many years in a clean, forgotten a "stochastic" direction in real economy, *an idea whose time must come.*

As supporting evidence, we had read papers which periodically loomed in the public scene with appeals for "dramatic change in the economy", warnings about "informational chaos", etc. (*Wall Street Journal, New York Times, Time, Fortune, The Economist, Business Week, Control Engineering, Datamation, IEEE Spectrum, Electrical World, Quality Progress*, etc.).

"Users want something that works" (Control Engineering, July 1989). And the last silent scream is: *Macroeconomics: The Enemy Within*, about noneffective econometric models and the software crisis in personal computer economic programming [30].

We hereby formulate the main results that have been extracted from this 23-year study:

(1)   The new philosophical background: disclosure of the Voltage Paradox, as the only tool for an adequate (not

116

intuitive) statistical-economic research for an individ-ual and social group economic (rational) behavior study;

(2) The 3D standard model of rational behavior (**SMRB**) construction:

(a) An essential time-dependent stochastic/digital/dis-crete model with **four saddle points**/local optimums.

(b) Its stability (feedback) and utility axiomatic treatment.

(c) Its only two linear-discrete standard procedures (sim-plex and regression) for each social 6-hour data file, separately.

(d) Standard software/code for standard digital protocol.

We suppose that these results offer a canonic solution to von Neumann-Morgenstern's and Wiener's classic problems.

(3) Any stable recurrent (economic) analog signal di-chotomies (two valid: vital and behavioristic -- functional control loops);

(4) A transition to common metric practice fractional ex-pectation assessment (discrete Sum or Mean with probabilistic feedback), as a silent fact of any meas-ured signal's cardinal utility (within its statistical-economic criterion).

(5) An engineering statement (theory-life compromise): Formulation of the Stability and Utility engineering concept for standard computing (an initial postulate and 12 axioms); the background for **EWIT** protocol (electronic "wheel" information technology) with standard digital software (or "digital nerve system"), including the two-period a day standard frequency of **macroeconomic** processes ("**macro soft**") or **four equal social half-periods a day** (Fig. 4). This can be treated as "semantic modeling" of a data base [21].

The final practical result (US patents: **5,515,288**; **5,732,193**; **S/N08/035,699**, pending), which is not presented here, is a full digital discrete image (protocol) of the 3D stochastic **SMRB** or "Stability and Utility" engineering concept. Thus, *thanks to modern electronic tools* (<u>central mainframe computer and microprocessor-based dedicated logical data controllers after each metering instrument</u>), the "linear-discrete" ideas of this monograph can be fully realized as distributed automation protocol in a production service oriented economy and social life with great benefits [41, 42, 43] [20].

EWIT is a *"big balloon."* In other words: <u>Beware of **PC** in line-recurrent industry</u>. **EWIT**'s importance is no less than the invention of the AC 3-phase rotating field by N. Tesla one hundred years ago. Within ten years, free people could be living in a different, more attractive, mainly "paperless" world, if total bureaucracy or "human factor" savagery does not ultimately win out. "Earth in the Balance" needs urgent protection [31].

We hope that this short book is a timely message to the bewildered reader, who is concerned with the truly conceptual aspects of the <u>measurement-based macroeconomy</u>; and to the professional, who is wary of fatal results due to the global-pretended **PC**'s inevitable *misinformation* concerning 3D data, which is the central cause of economic, ecological, and social ills for billions of the boiling majority at the phony "high-tech" end of the twentieth horrendous century [21].

---

[20] It is wise to remember that an adequate information is money [22].

[21] It seems to us that the most significant <u>economic</u> result of the **PC** market (Internet) will be "Club Kasparov" commercial activity. The "knowledge workers" or programmers' new economy (<u>microbusiness</u>) and our subject: nonprogrammable-general-digital cybertech-automatic line basic ("old") industrial economy (<u>macrobusiness</u>) are two completely different fields (**with different information technologies**).

5.7 About the Author

The author holds a Ph.D. from the Academy of Municipal Economy (Moscow); and is a P.E at the Israel Electric Corporation Ltd.; Member, Consultant and Lecturer in some professional associates, projects and educational organizations; author of numerous monographs, papers and discussions presented at local, regional, national and two **IEEE** international conventions.

The author is a practicing electrical engineer in AC service voltage quality and industrial data processing with 42-years experience in the electrical supply field.

He does not like plenary sessions and elegant rituals; he does not trust imposing orators or the productivity of verbal discussions.

He believes in the reiterative reading of written evidence and instrumental records (the monotonous process: charts and histograms), i.e., in silent facts. He believes in the power of long-term thinking regarding simple events (Plato was right).

REFERENCES

Selected Works

1. Energy Security Report to the President, U.S. DOE, 1987.

2. **von Neumann J.** and **Morgenstern O.** (1944), *Theory of Games and Economic Behavior*, 1st Science Ed., Princeton Univ. Press, 1944.

3. **Wiener N.** (1947), *Cybernetics and Society*, 2nd print., London, 1954.

4. *Selected Papers on Noise and Stochastic Processes* (1954), edited by **N. Wax**, Dover Publ. Inc., NY.

5. **Ailleret P.** (1956), *Bull. Soc. Francaise des Electr. de France*, № 1.

6. **Arrow K.** et al. (1958), *Studies in linear and nonlinear programming*, Stanford University Press, CA.

7. **Allen R.** (1960) *Mathematical Economics*, 2nd ed., Macmillan Co. Ltd., NY.

8. **Forrester J.** (1961), *Industrial Dynamics*, MIT Press, Cambridge, MA.

9. **Friedman** (1962), *Capitalism and Freedom*, Chicago Univ. Press.

10. **Klein L.** (1962), *An Introduction to Econometrics*, Prentice-Hall Int. Inc., NY.

11. **Baumol W.** (1962), *Economic Theory and Operations Analysis*, Prentice-Hall Int. Inc., London.

12. **Dantzig G.** (1963), *Linear Programming and Extensions*, RAND, Princeton.

13. **Bary C.** (1963), *Operational Economics of Electric Utilities*, Columbia University Press, New York – London.

14. **Seligman B.** (1963), *Main Currents in Modern Economics since 1870*. The Free Press of Glencoe, NY.

15. **Hadley G.** (1964), *Nonlinear and dynamic programming*, Chicago Univ. Press.

16. **Young L.** (1969), *Lectures on the Calculus of Variations and Optimal Control Theory*, Sounders Co., London.

17. **Pelissier R.** (1975), *Les reseaux d'energie electrique*, Dunod, Paris.

18. **Pervozvanski A.** (1975) *Mathematical Models in Production Control*, Science PH, Moscow.

19. **Aberson M.** (1975), *Voltage Control Optimization*, Energy PH, Moscow.

20. **Crew M.** and **Kleindorfer P.** (1979), *Public Utility Economics*, St. Martin Press, NY.

21. **Date C.** (1986), *An Introduction to Data Base Systems*, 4th ed., Addison-Wesley Publ. Co., Menlo Park, CA.

22. **Dordick H.** (1986), *Understanding Modern Telecommunications*, McGraw-Hill, Inc., NY.

23. **Bertsekas D., Gallager R.** (1987) *Data Networks* (MIT), Prentice-Hall Int. Inc., NY.

24. **Peters T.** (1989) Tomorrow's Companies, *The Economist*, March 4-10, 1989, p. 27.

25. Report WG 36-05 (1989), *Voltage Unbalance, Dips and Fluctuations*, Electra (CIGRE), 1989, №. 123.

122

26. **Leff H.**, et al. (1990) *Maxwell's Demon: entropy, informa-tion, computing*, Princeton UP.

27. *Utility and Probability* (1990) edited by **J. Eatwell, M. Milgate, P. Newman**, Norton, PH, NY – London.

28. **Harvey A.** (1990), *The Econometric Analysis of Time Se-ries*, Simon and Schuster Int., London – NY.

29. **Rose F.** (1990) A New Age for Business? *Fortune*, Oct. 8, 1990, N22.

30. **Wanniski J.** (1991), Macroeconomics: The Enemy Within, *The Wall Street Journal*, Europe, July 2, 1991, p. 10.

31. **Gore A.** (1993), *Earth in the Balance*, A Plume Book, NY.

32. **Romanchik D.** (1994) What Do You Do with All That Data? *Test & Measurement World*, Feb. 15, 1994, p. 22.

33. **Walsh J.** (1994) Will the Jobs Ever Come Back? *Time Int.*, February 7, 1994, p. 27.

34. **Henney A.** (1994) *El. supply privatization in England*, EEE Ltd., London.

35. **Marks J.** (1994), An international computer protocol stan-dard is essential, *Power Eng.*, Feb. 94, pp. 36-37.

36. **Wharmby B.** (1995) The Future of Information Technol-ogy, *Electricity International*, November 1995.

37. **Merlin A.** (1996), *Symposium CIGRE*, Helsinki: Electra №164, pp. 8-10.

38. **Uchitelle L.** (1996) What Has the Computer Done for Us Lately? *The New York Times Weekly Review*, December 8, 1996, p. 1.

39. **Kirkpatrick D.** (1998) Microsoft: Is Your Company Its Next Meal? *Fortune*, April 27, 1998, p. 92.

40. **Bylinsky G.** (1998), Industry Wakes Up to the Year 2000 Menace, *Fortune*, April 27, 1998, p. 163.

41. **Aberson M.** (1996), An object-oriented real-time open protocol (EWIT), *IEEE Conference*, Jerusalem, pp. 25-28.

42. **Aberson M.** (1997), Smart Meter's Protocol, *Energy-Mart.'97 Conference*, Chicago (abstracts).

43. **Aberson M.** (1998), *Smart Meter's Protocol*, IEEE, Melecon-98, Tel-Aviv, pp. 293-297.

44. **Warsh D.** (1999), *One Big Wave, Come and Gone*, The Boston Globe (business section), May 16, 1999, Boston, MA.

Resume of Dr. Michael E. Aberson

Education:

1989   Dorset Business School (G.B.), Management Consulting Program.

1964-1967   Ph.D. in Power Distribution & Consumption, Academy of Science, Moscow, USSR. Dissertation: *"Optimization of Voltage Control in Distribution Networks and Reactive Loads in Urban Electricity."* Thesis Directors: Academician B. Gnedenko (Moscow University, Math), Academician V. Pugachov (Institute of Program's Control, Department of Random Processes), Academician V. Popkov (Electrical Sciences), and Prof. Yakov Chervonenkis.

1947-1954   MSc. In Electrical Engineering, Institute of Transport, Moscow.

Professional Experience:

1986-1997   Israel Electric Corporation, Haifa, Israel
Manager, Research and Development Group
Managed Projects:
- Digital Data Protocol
- Static Stability Management
- Networks 22kV Protection
- Voltage Economic Optimization

1964-1985   Academy of Science, Department of Municipal Economy, Moscow, USSR
Project Manager
Managed Projects:
- Fundamentals of National Standards.
- Probability and Statistical Analysis of Voltage.
- Economical Regulation of Voltage and Reactive Loads in Urban Areas.
- Damage and Service of Voltage Regime for Urban Consumers.

1958-1964	National Institute of Heavy Industry and Electrical Equipment
	Senior Manager, Division of Electrical Supply
	Designed, calculated, and chose schemes for projects:
	• Electrical Supply for Iron and Steel Plant, Ceylon
	• Electrical Supply for Bao Tou Steel Industry Complex, China
	• Electrical Supply for Helwan Steel Industry Complex, Egypt.

U.S. Patents:

1998	"Method and Apparatus for Behavioristic-Format Coding of Quantitative Resource Data: Distributed Automation Protocol"
1996	"Method and Control Apparatus for Generating Analog Recurrent Signal Security Data Feedback"
1995	"Method and Apparatus for Behavioristic-Format Coding of Qualitative Analog Data: Distributed Automation Protocol"

Publications: Dr. Michael Aberson is chief author of 110 publications: 1 monograph, 7 books, 43 articles, and other articles that were written with co-authors. Some examples are listed below.

1998	"Smart Meter's Protocol", *IEEE*, Conference Proceedings, Tel-Aviv, Israel, pp. 293 – 297.
1996	"An Object Oriented Real-Time Open Protocol", *IEEE*, XIX Conference Proceedings, Jerusalem, Israel, pp. 25-28.
1976	Book: "Control of the Dead Zone and Voltage Quality", Academy of Science, Moscow, USSR.
1975	Monograph: "Voltage Control Optimization", "Energy" Publishing House, Moscow, USSR.
1972	Book: "Urban Networks: Principles and Economy", Academy of Science, Moscow, USSR.

Professional Activities:

1979-1986	Council of Ministries, USSR, Fellow, The Science Committee "Quality of Electrical Energy"
1975-1980	International Electrotechnical Commission (IEC), Fellow, USSR Section.
1979	US-USSR Electrical Network Conference. Lecturer, "The Urban Engineering Network".
1964-1979	Non-staff editor and reviewer, "Electricity", and "Industrial Energetic" Journals, Moscow, USSR.

Consulting:

1974-1985	The State Committee of Standards, Moscow, USSR.
1965-1976	National Network Research and Project Institute, Moscow, USSR.
1966-1978	The State Project Institute for Urban Energetic, Moscow, USSR.

Awards:

1976	The Ministry of Energetic, USSR, First Prize: "Regulations for Voltage Control in Operating of the Urban Electrical Networks".
1972	Ministry of Energetic, USSR, Honorary Award: "Improvement of Voltage Regime in Russia".

The United States of America

*A*s to industrial management update and macrobusiness productivity, its high-tech is 3D standard model of rational behavior (*Fig. 4*): canonic time-digital soft-ware source (code) for ultimate chips of each metering instrument (three US patents). It presents 3D SMRB decomposition in standard matrix information technology for any macrobusiness unit and sector as a whole (EWIT protocol and Cybernet).

Unemployment and spare time problems are solved automatically via standard 6-hour shift and EWIT protocol money, first of all for the industrial world.

Personal computer is the next "Panama" for high-tech market in industry automation history (Cybernetics). It is useful in microbusiness sector, only.

M. Aberson, the author,
2000

128